Food

Titles in the
Discovering Careers
series

Adventure
Animals
Art
Computers
Construction
Environment
Fashion
Food
Health
Math
Movies
Nature
Performing Arts
Science
Space Exploration
Sports
Transportation
Writing

DISCOVERING CAREERS

Food

Ferguson's
An Infobase Learning Company

Food

Ferguson's
An imprint of Infobase Learning
132 West 31st Street
New York NY 10001

Library of Congress Cataloging-in-Publication Data

Food.
    p. cm — (Discovering careers series)
    Includes bibliographical references and index.
    ISBN-13: 978-0-8160-8057-1 (hardcover : alk. paper)
    ISBN-10: 0-8160-8057-7 (hardcover : alk. paper) 1. Food service—Vocational guidance—Juvenile literature. 2. Food industry and trade—Vocational guidance—Juvenile literature.   I. Ferguson Publishing.
    TX911.3.V62F65   2011
    647.95023—dc23
                                2011022916

Ferguson's books are available at special discounts when purchased in bulk quantities for businesses, associations, institutions, or sales promotions. Please call our Special Sales Department in New York at (212) 967-8800 or (800) 322-8755.

You can find Ferguson's on the World Wide Web
at http://www.infobaselearning.com

Text design by Erika K. Arroyo and Erik Lindstrom
Composition by Erik Lindstrom
Cover printed by IBT Global, Troy, N.Y.
Book printed and bound by IBT Global, Troy, N.Y.
Date printed: November 2011
Printed in the United States of America

10 9 8 7 6 5 4 3 2 1

This book is printed on acid-free paper.

CONTENTS

Introduction

You may not have decided yet what you want to be in the future. And you don't have to decide right away. You do know that right now you are interested in careers in the food industry. Do any of the statements below describe you? If so, you may want to begin thinking about what a career in the food industry might mean for you.

___ I enjoy reading about food and its history.

___ I enjoy cooking for my friends and family.

___ I like to write stories.

___ I like to teach others.

___ I like to discover new restaurants or kinds of food and tell my friends about them.

___ I enjoy planting a garden.

___ I am responsible for feeding and caring for our family pet.

___ I enjoy coming up with my own recipes.

___ I belong to a 4-H Club or the National FFA Organization.

___ My parents are farmers and I would like to continue the family business.

___ I enjoy conducting experiments.

___ I collect specimens to view under my microscope.

___ I like to fish.

___ I am fascinated by all of the different types of food in the world.

___ I enjoy learning about healthy and unhealthy foods.

___ I like to give directions to other people.

1

Discovering Careers: Food is a book about careers in the food industry, from bakery industry workers to farmers to supermarket managers. Careers in this field can be found on farms, in factories, in publishing companies, in classrooms, in business offices, in restaurants, on ships, in wineries and breweries, in supermarkets, and in countless other settings.

This book describes many possibilities for future careers in the food industry. Read through it and see how the different careers are connected. For example, if you are interested in working outdoors, you should read the articles on Farmers, Fishers, and Grain Merchants, as well as other entries in this book. If you are interested in cooking, you will want to read about Cooking Instructors, Cooks and Chefs, as well as other entries in this book. If you are interested in writing about food, you will want to read about Cookbook and Recipe Writers, Food Writers and Editors, and other careers. If you are interested in the manufacturing and production aspects of this field, you will want to read about Confectionery Industry Workers and other careers. If you are interested in learning more about the science of food, you should read Food Technologists. Go ahead and explore!

What Do Food Industry Workers Do?

The first section of each chapter begins with a heading such as "What Dietitians and Nutritionists Do" or "What Winemakers Do." It tells what it's like to work at this job. It describes typical responsibilities and assignments. You will find out about working conditions. Which workers are employed on farms? Which ones work at computers in offices? Which ones work in schools? This section answers these and other questions.

How Do I Become a Food Industry Worker?

The section called "Education and Training" tells you what schooling you need for employment in each job—a high school diploma, training at a junior college, a college degree, or more. It also talks about on-the-job training that you can expect to receive after you're hired, and whether or not you must complete an apprenticeship program.

How Much Do Food Industry Workers Earn?

The "Earnings" section gives salary figures for the job described in the chapter. These figures give you a general idea of how much money people with this job can make. Keep in mind that many people really earn more or less than the amounts given here because actual salaries depend on many different things, such as the size of the company, the location of the company, and the amount of education, training, and experience you have. Generally, but not always, bigger companies located in major cities pay more than smaller ones in smaller cities and towns, and people with more education, training, and experience earn more. Also remember that these figures are current or recent salaries. They will probably be different by the time you are ready to enter the workforce.

What Will the Future Be Like for Food Industry Workers?

The "Outlook" section discusses the employment outlook for the career: whether the total number of people employed in this career will increase or decrease in the coming years and whether jobs in this field will be easy or hard to find. These predictions are based on economic conditions, the size and makeup of the population, foreign competition, and new technology. They come from the U.S. Department of Labor, professional associations, and other sources.

Keep in mind that these predictions are general statements. No one knows for sure what the future will be like. Also remember that the employment outlook is a general statement about an industry and does not necessarily apply to everyone. A determined and talented person may be able to find a job in an industry or career with the worst outlook. And a person without ambition and the proper training will find it difficult to find a job in even a booming industry or career field.

Where Can I Find More Information?

Each chapter includes a sidebar called "For More Info." It lists resources that you can contact to find out more about the field and careers in the field. You will find names, addresses, phone numbers, e-mail addresses, and Web sites of food-oriented associations and organizations.

Extras

Every chapter has a few extras. There are photos that show food workers in action. There are sidebars and notes on ways to explore the field, fun facts, profiles of people in the field, and lists of Web sites and books that might be helpful. At the end of the book you will find three additional sections: "Glossary," "Browse and Learn More," and "Index." The Glossary gives brief definitions of words that relate to education, career training, or employment that you may be unfamiliar with. The Browse and Learn More section lists food-related books, periodicals, and Web sites to explore. The Index includes all the job titles mentioned in the book.

It's not too soon to think about your future. We hope you discover several possible career choices in the food industry. Happy hunting!

Bakery Industry Workers

What Bakery Industry Workers Do

Bakery industry workers make bread, cakes, biscuits, pies, pastries, crackers, and other baked goods in commercial, institutional (schools, hospitals, etc.), and industrial bakeries.

Most bakery industry workers working for manufacturers (for example, a large company that produces hamburger buns or coffee cakes) participate in only some of the steps involved in creating a baked item. These workers, known as *food batchmakers,* are usually designated by the type of machine they operate or the stage of baking with which they are involved.

In preparing the dough or batter for goods baked in an industrial bakery, different workers make the different components. *Blenders* tend machines that blend flour. Skilled technicians known as *broth mixers* control flour sifters and various vats to measure and mix liquid solutions for fermenting, oxidizing, and shortening. These solutions consist of such ingredients as yeast, sugar, shortening, and enriching ingredients mixed with water or milk. *Batter mixers* tend machines that mix ingredients for batters for cakes and other products. Other kinds of mixers and shapers include *unleavened-dough mixers, sweet-goods-machine operators,* and *pretzel twisters.*

Cracker-and-cookie-machine operators roll dough into sheets and form crackers or cookies before baking. *Wafer-machine operators* perform similar tasks with wafer batter. *Batter scalers* operate machines that deposit measured amounts of

EXPLORING

- Visit the Home Baking Association's Web site, http://www.homebaking.org, for tips on baking and a useful glossary of terms.
- In addition to school courses, take baking or cooking classes that are offered locally by community centers, grocery stores, or tech schools.
- Ask your teacher or parent to help you arrange for a tour of a local bakery and talk to workers about their jobs.

- If there is a cooking school in your area, visit it and meet with the teachers to discuss this line of work.
- If you are in high school, you may be able to get a part-time or summer job at a neighborhood bakery. Although you may only be responsible for taking customers' orders and ringing up sales, you will be able to experience working in this environment.

batter on conveyors. *Doughnut makers* and *doughnut-machine operators* mix batter, shape, and fry doughnuts.

Bakery helpers grease pans, move supplies, measure dump materials, and clean equipment. They may also fill, slice, package, seal, stack, or count baked goods.

When baked goods are ready for delivery and sale, *bakery checkers* distribute them to *route-sales drivers*. These workers deliver products to customers and try to drum up new business or increase business along their routes. Bakeries also employ *bakery-maintenance engineers*, also called *bakery-machine mechanics* or *plant mechanics*, to keep the many mixers, ovens, and other machines in good working order.

Bakery supervisors, who work in industrial bakeries, are sometimes assisted by bakers or all-around bakers in managing

A pastry chef prepares a dessert. (Michael Sofronski, The Image Works)

production. Bakers and all-around bakers, however, most frequently work in small businesses, hotels, or restaurants where they develop recipes and mix, shape, bake, and finish baked goods.

Bread and pastry bakers, also known as *pastry chefs,* work in restaurants, small businesses, such as neighborhood bakeries, and institutions, such as schools. Unlike bakery workers employed in industrial settings, these bakers and chefs often do much of their work by hand. They may have a fair amount of independence in deciding what items and how much of them

Tips for Success

To be a successful bakery industry worker, you should

- be able to work well with your hands
- have artistic ability if you are required to decorate cakes, cookies, doughnuts, and other baked goods
- be able to work well as part of a team
- have strong communication skills
- have a keen sense of smell and taste
- be willing to work a variety of shifts, including those on nights and weekends

to produce. Creativity is needed, especially when decorating an item made for a special occasion, such as a birthday cake for Bobby or a wedding cake for John and Jane.

Education and Training

Most employers prefer to hire high school graduates. There are many high school classes that will help you prepare for this field. Family and consumer science will teach you about food preparation. Health classes will educate you about nutrition and sanitation. Math classes, such as algebra and geometry, will help you to become comfortable working with numbers and making calculations. You may also want to take science courses such as biology and chemistry to get an understanding of the properties and reactions of different substances such as yeast. If you are interested in working as a bakery-maintenance engineer, take shop classes that will teach you to work with electricity and machinery.

Some bakery industry workers obtain useful skills through education in technical schools or in the U.S. military. However, they usually complete their education on the job. In some companies, bakery workers can learn through formal apprenticeships. Apprenticeships consist of a blend of classroom and on-the-job instruction and take several years to complete.

Earnings

Salaries for bakery industry workers vary widely due to factors such as size and type of employer, the employee's experience, and job title. According to the U.S. Department of Labor, the median yearly earnings for all bakers were $23,450 in 2010. Salaries ranged from less than $17,000 to $37,000 or more.

DID YOU KNOW?

Where Bakery Industry Workers Work

- Bakery departments in supermarkets
- Hospitals
- Manufacturing plants
- Restaurants and hotels
- Schools
- Small retail bakeries
- Wholesale bakeries

FOR MORE INFO

For information on training, contact
AIB International
PO Box 3999
Manhattan, KS 66505-3999
800-633-5137
http://www.aibonline.org

For industry information, contact
American Bakers Association
1300 I Street, NW, Suite 700 West
Washington, DC 20005-7203

202-789-0300
http://www.americanbakers.org

For industry information, contact
American Society of Baking
PO Box 336
Swedesboro, NJ 08085-0336
800-713-0462
info@asbe.org
http://www.asbe.org

Outlook

Employment for bakery industry workers will only be fair during the next decade. The increasing use of automated equipment and processes has decreased the number of jobs that are available. However, employment will be better for bakery workers at retail locations because of the growing number of traditional bakeries and specialty shops, such as cookie, muffin, and bagel shops. Additionally, many positions will become available as workers retire or change jobs.

Brewers

What Brewers Do

Brewers make beer, an alcoholic beverage that, in the United States, people age 21 and over can drink legally. Brewers have many job duties. They select the exact blend and kind of flavoring hops to regulate the number of minutes the wort boils. There are guidelines for each style of beer, but within those guidelines the brewer may experiment to create a truly unique taste.

There are more than 50 styles of beer, but the four basic ingredients of all beers are malted barley, hops, yeast, and water. Brewers grind the malted barley in special machines so that its husk is removed and the kernel broken. Next, they add a precise amount of water and raise the temperature to dissolve the natural sugars, starches, and enzymes of the barley. To complete the mashing process, the brewer strains out the barley grains. The remaining sweetened liquid, called malt extract, is now ready to become the wort, which is concentrated, unhopped beer. The brewer transfers the wort from the mashing vessel to a brewing kettle, where boiling hops are added. The hopped wort is boiled. After it has cooled, the hop leaves or pellet residue are removed in a process called sparging, and the wort is now ready for its most vital ingredient, yeast. When the yeast is added, the fermentation process begins.

After the desired time for the primary fermentation, the brewer transfers the beer to a lagering kettle, a container where the beer is allowed to age. The fermentation continues but at a

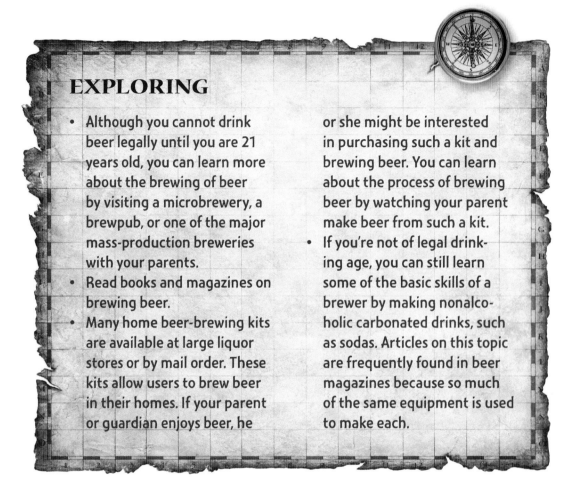

EXPLORING

- Although you cannot drink beer legally until you are 21 years old, you can learn more about the brewing of beer by visiting a microbrewery, a brewpub, or one of the major mass-production breweries with your parents.
- Read books and magazines on brewing beer.
- Many home beer-brewing kits are available at large liquor stores or by mail order. These kits allow users to brew beer in their homes. If your parent or guardian enjoys beer, he or she might be interested in purchasing such a kit and brewing beer. You can learn about the process of brewing beer by watching your parent make beer from such a kit.
- If you're not of legal drinking age, you can still learn some of the basic skills of a brewer by making nonalcoholic carbonated drinks, such as sodas. Articles on this topic are frequently found in beer magazines because so much of the same equipment is used to make each.

slower pace. After the desired aging or maturation of the beer, anywhere from two weeks to several months, the beer is again transferred to a storage tank, where it is ready to be bottled.

Brewers add carbonation to their beers either by injecting carbon dioxide (a gas) into the storage tank just before the beer is to be bottled or kegged or by adding a priming sugar, usually dry malt extract or corn sugar diluted in boiled water.

Some *craftbrewers* at microbreweries may also help bottle their beer. At small breweries, craftbrewers frequently sterilize their tanks, kettles, hoses, and other brewing equipment. This

A brewer collects a sample from a brewing vat. (Jeff Greenberg, The Image Works)

keeps bacteria and other harmful substances from growing on them. Brewers who have the right resources and live in the right environment may grow, harvest, and store their own hops. But a brewer's primary duty is always to brew beer, to experiment and come up with new recipes, and to seek out the right ingredients for the particular style of beer that is being brewed.

Most brewers are content to remain *masterbrewer* of a microbrewery or brewpub, but some may advance to management positions if the opportunity arises. *Brewery managers* oversee the day-to-day operations of a brewery. They manage finances,

DID YOU KNOW?

- Beer is one of the oldest alcoholic beverages known to humanity. It has been brewed for approximately 8,000 years.
- Beer brewing in the United States began in the 1630s.
- Ninety to 95 percent of beer is water.

create advertising campaigns, and hire and fire employees.

Education and Training

High school classes in biology, chemistry, and math will be particularly useful if you are interested in becoming a brewer. Classes in biochemistry and microbiology will prepare you for the more specialized aspects of brewing that serious craftbrewers must master. You will need a background in science and math to be able to perform basic brewing and engineering calculations and to follow technical discussions on brewing topics.

Employers today prefer to hire only brewers who have completed some kind of formal training program in brewing sciences, or who have had extensive apprenticeship training at another brewery. See the sources at the end of this article for information on training programs. A college degree is not required for admission to the professional brewing programs, but you will need to complete college course work in biological sciences (biology, biochemistry, microbiology), chemistry, physics, math (precalculus), and engineering.

Earnings

Salaries for those in the brewing business vary considerably based on several factors, including the exact position a person holds, the size of the brewery, its location, the popularity of its beer, and the length of time the brewery has been in business. Brewers running their own microbreweries or brewpubs, like any small business owner, may have very low take-home wages for several years as the business becomes established. Earnings could possibly range from nothing to $20,000 or so. Head brew-

Words to Learn

barley a cereal grain used in beer-making

fermentation a process in which ingredients in food- or beverage-making undergo a chemical process

hops the dried flower of the female hop plant

mash a mix of grains and water that is used to make wort

mashing process a step during brewing that creates wort

wort a liquid formed by soaking mash in hot water

yeast a type of fungi that is used to help make bread and some alcoholic beverages

zymurgy the science of fermentation

ers and masterbrewers with a couple years of professional experience and working for a brewery may have earnings that range from $30,000 to $65,000. A brewer's salary can increase with bonuses or profit sharing if the brewery does well in the course of a year.

Outlook

Beer is a popular alcoholic beverage. Major brewers such as Miller, Anheuser Busch, and Coors have taken notice of the craftbrewing trend by introducing their own premium-style beers.

Although craftbrewing accounts for only about 3 to 5 percent of the U.S. beer market, it is a growing segment of the beer industry. According to the Association of Brewers, there are now more than 1,500 microbreweries, brewpubs, and regional specialty breweries operating across the country. As people have become accustomed to the availability of unique tasting beers, they have created a growing market for these products. There is a strong demand for skilled brewers. Those with training should have the best opportunities.

FOR MORE INFO

For information on craftbrewing and apprenticeships, contact
American Brewers Guild
1001 Maple Street
Salisbury, VT 05769-9445
800-636-1331
abg@abgbrew.com
http://www.abgbrew.com

For information on professional brewing and homebrewing and related publications, contact
Brewers Association
PO Box 1679
Boulder, CO 80306-1679

303-447-0816
info@brewersassociation.org
http://www.brewersassociation.org

For information on courses and the diploma in brewing technology, contact
Siebel Institute of Technology & World Brewing Academy
1777 North Clybourn Avenue
Chicago, IL 60614-5520
312-255-0705
info@siebelinstitute.com
http://www.siebelinstitute.com

Canning and Preserving Industry Workers

What Canning and Preserving Industry Workers Do

Canning and preserving industry workers monitor equipment and perform routine tasks in food-processing plants that can, preserve, and quick-freeze such foods as vegetables, fruits, frozen dinners, jams, jellies, preserves, pickles, and soups. They also process and preserve seafood, including shrimp, oysters, crabs, clams, and fish.

In large plants, each worker may do one specific task. In smaller plants, one worker may do many of the tasks necessary to preserve the food.

In order to operate successfully, a food-processing plant must have plenty of the foodstuff it processes. Some of the major tasks performed by workers outside of processing plants include arranging with farmers to grow certain kinds of food crops for processing; negotiating with farmers concerning price, the quantity that will be delivered, and the quality standards that the crop must meet; and purchasing raw materials and other goods for processing.

When food arrives at the processing plant, workers examine and record its quality, or grade, and mark it for separation by class, size, color, and condition. Then they unload it for processing.

Although most processing of food is done with automatic machines, workers are still needed to operate machinery; in-

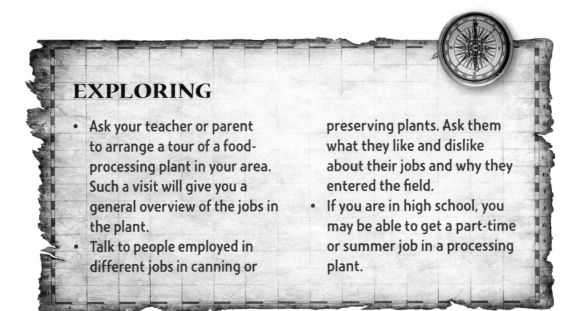

EXPLORING

- Ask your teacher or parent to arrange a tour of a food-processing plant in your area. Such a visit will give you a general overview of the jobs in the plant.
- Talk to people employed in different jobs in canning or preserving plants. Ask them what they like and dislike about their jobs and why they entered the field.
- If you are in high school, you may be able to get a part-time or summer job in a processing plant.

spect, unload, sort, and wash food; measure ingredients, and monitor production processes. Plants that process fish and shellfish need workers to kill, prepare, and clean the fish before processing.

Next, foods are processed. They may be cooked, blanched (scalded with hot water or steam), deep-fried, pickled (soaked in a salt or vinegar solution), smoked, frozen, or dehydrated (removing all the water). No matter the process, workers are needed to prepare food for these processes and operate equipment during the process.

Other foods, including many vegetables, are processed after they have been sealed in cans. Workers are needed to fill cans or jars with food to specified volume and weight and operate closing machines to put an airtight seal on the containers. By keeping as much air out of the container as possible, the food will stay fresh longer.

Once food has been processed and packaged, it is labeled, tested, and inspected. Workers test and inspect cans, jars, and other packaging to ensure that they are sealed correctly and do not contain foreign materials.

Managers of all types are needed to monitor and coordinate the activities of workers. They hire and fire employees, train workers, contact buyers, coordinate maintenance and operation of plant machinery, and meet with other managers to discuss production goals and other issues.

Education and Training

To prepare for this career, take high school classes in math, science, family and consumer science, English, and computer science. Many food-processing jobs have no minimum educational requirements, although most employers prefer to hire high school graduates. You will need at least a high school diploma if you want to become a manager. Beginners seldom need previous experience, and usually they can learn their jobs quickly. Generally there is up to one month of on-the-job training.

Many plants provide orientation sessions for new workers and programs on safety and sanitation. For those who want to be managers, a college degree is recommended, with studies in accounting, management, and other business courses as well as chemistry.

Earnings

Although some products can be processed at any time during the year, the level of activity in many food-processing plants varies with the season, and earnings of workers vary accordingly. Larger plants overcome the seasonality of their food products by maintaining large inventories of raw foodstuffs, and workers in these plants generally work full time throughout the year.

DID YOU KNOW?

- The first frozen food products were created by Clarence Birdseye in the 1930s.
- 94 percent of shoppers have purchased frozen food.
- Frozen dinners/entrees are the most popular frozen food.
- Approximately 1.5 million people are employed in the food manufacturing industry.

Sources: American Frozen Food Institute, Tupperware Corporation, U.S. Department of Labor

Profile: Nicolas Appert (1749–1841)

Nicolas Appert, a Frenchman, invented what we consider modern canning techniques in the late 1700s. During the Napoleonic Wars, more soldiers were falling ill or dying due to scurvy (a disease caused by an absence of Vitamin C in the body), malnutrition (poor nutrition because of a lack of food or a poor diet), and starvation than from enemy soldiers. To combat this problem, the French government offered a reward to the person who could find a way to preserve food. Appert, a brewer, baker, and candy-maker, experimented for 14 years until he realized that food could be preserved by putting it into bottles, corking them, and submerging them in boiling water. Voilá! Food spoilage became much less of a problem, and Appert became a rich man due to his creativity and willingness to try for years to find a solution to a problem.

Source: Grocery Manufacturers Association

Earnings for workers in the canning and preserving industry vary widely. Many positions, especially at the entry level, pay little more than the minimum wage ($7.25 an hour). Experienced workers typically earn salaries that range from $20,000 to $30,000, while managers have earnings that range from $40,000 to $80,000 or more annually.

Generally, seasonal workers earn an hourly wage; some, particularly those working on processing ships or for canneries in Alaska, also receive board and lodging. Benefits vary from company to company.

Outlook

The use of automated equipment and computer technology throughout the food-processing industry means that fewer people will be needed to process, preserve, and can foods. Wherever it is efficient and cost effective, machines will take over the tasks that people have been doing. Therefore, overall

FOR MORE INFO

For facts and statistics about frozen food, contact
American Frozen Food Institute
2000 Corporate Ridge Boulevard, Suite 1000
McLean, VA 22102-7862
703-821-0770
info@affi.com
http://www.affi.com

For consumer fact sheets, information on issues in the food science industry, and food safety news, visit the association's Web site or contact
Grocery Manufacturers Association
1350 I Street, NW, Suite 300
Washington, DC 20005-3377

202-639-5900
info@gmaonline.org
http://www.gmaonline.org

For information on careers and education, contact
Institute of Food Technologists
525 West Van Buren, Suite 1000
Chicago, IL 60607-3830
312-782-8424
info@ift.org
http://www.ift.org

employment in the industry is expected to decline over the next several years. Researchers and technical workers with specialized expertise and college-level training will have the best employment opportunities.

In some kinds of food processing, such as the fish canneries in Alaska, employment levels are related to weather and other natural factors that vary from year to year.

Caterers

What Caterers Do

Caterers plan, prepare, and serve meals to large groups of people. They help organize parties, formal dinners, wedding receptions, and a variety of other gatherings. Caterers may be involved with all aspects of a celebration, such as planning the menu, buying the food and drinks, preparing the food, and supervising the food service.

In addition to preparing food, caterers must also be able to make a room look special. They use flowers, wall hangings, streamers, and other decorations to make an area attractive. Caterers also set up the tables and chairs and provide the table-cloths, silverware, dishes, and napkins. A large catering company may organize as many as 50 or more events a month.

If handling a large banquet in a hotel or other location, the caterer will usually prepare the food at the hotel. The caterer might also work in a customer's kitchen if the affair is going to be at the customer's home. In both of these cases, it is important for the caterer to visit the site of the function well before the date of the event. This will help the caterer decide how and where the food will be prepared. Caterers may also prepare the food in their own kitchens or in a mobile kitchen. In all cases, frequent phone contact is often necessary to organize events.

The caterer and customer will usually work together within a set price range that they have agreed on. The caterer will develop a menu and atmosphere that the customer can enjoy.

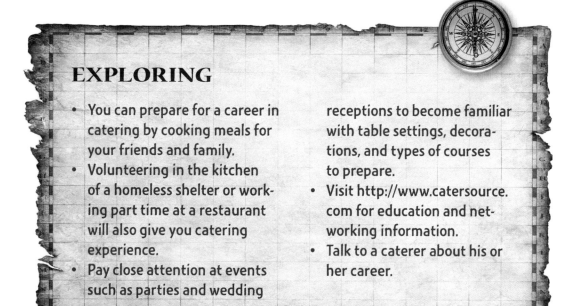

EXPLORING

- You can prepare for a career in catering by cooking meals for your friends and family.
- Volunteering in the kitchen of a homeless shelter or working part time at a restaurant will also give you catering experience.
- Pay close attention at events such as parties and wedding receptions to become familiar with table settings, decorations, and types of courses to prepare.
- Visit http://www.catersource.com for education and networking information.
- Talk to a caterer about his or her career.

Customers always want their affairs to be special, and the caterer's ability to keep customers happy will determine his or her success.

Caterers hire all of the staff that will work at an event. They make sure enough people show up to work all the tables and assist at the bar.

Education and Training

If you're interested in becoming a caterer, you should take classes in business, family and consumer science, and health.

Although many caterers have college training in baking, cooking, or business management, other caterers may have picked up their training outside of school at a restaurant or another catering company. When you become a caterer, you may

A caterer prepares a meal. (Rachel Epstein, The Image Works)

start off by serving food or cleaning the dishes at an event. You may also work as a chef's assistant or as an assistant business manager for the catering department of a hotel. No matter how you start out, to be a caterer you must feel comfortable with planning and preparing an event, being in charge of workers, and advertising your services.

The most successful caterers enter the industry through a formal training program. Vocational or community colleges often offer programs in food science, food preparation, and catering.

Tips for Success

To be a successful caterer, you should

- be outgoing and friendly
- be highly organized
- have good problem-solving skills
- be able to work under deadline pressure
- have excellent communication skills
- be willing to works nights and weekends

Earnings

Full-time caterers typically earn between $15,000 and $60,000 per year, depending on their skill level, reputation, and experience. An extremely successful caterer can easily earn more than $75,000 annually. A part-time caterer may earn $7,000 to $15,000 per year, subject to the same variables as a full-time caterer.

Outlook

Employment in food service should continue to be strong during the next decade. Opportunities will be good for individuals who handle special events, such as weddings, bar mitzvahs and bat mitzvahs, and other festive occasions, which are not as affected when the economy is not doing well. On the other hand, businesses may hold fewer catered events, such as luncheons, during times of recession and cutbacks.

There is a lot of competition for jobs because many hotels and restaurants now

DID YOU KNOW?

Where Caterers Work

Most caterers are self-employed, but they work for a variety of clients, including

- Airlines
- Banquet halls
- Corporations
- Country clubs
- Cruise ships
- Hotels
- Individuals/families
- Schools

FOR MORE INFO

For industry news, contact
**International Food Service Executives
Association**
4955 Miller Street, Suite 107
Wheat Ridge, CO 80033-2294
800-893-5499
http://www.ifsea.com

For industry information, contact
National Association of Catering Executives
9881 Broken Land Parkway, Suite 301
Columbia, MD 21046-3015
410-290-5410
http://www.nace.net

offer catering services. However, despite competition and ever-changing economic conditions, highly skilled and motivated caterers should be in demand throughout the country, especially in and around large cities.

Confectionery Industry Workers

What Confectionery Industry Workers Do

Confectionery industry workers manufacture and package sweets, including bonbons, hard and soft candy, stuffed dates, popcorn balls, and many other types of confections. The term *confectionery* is just another word for candy.

Confectionery industry workers operate machines to mix and cook candy ingredients, to form candy mixtures into shapes, and to package them for sale. Many different machines are used to make the molded, filled, pulled, whipped, and coated candies that Americans consume. Even when the candy-making production line is completely automated, workers still are needed to monitor the various processing steps. Some candy-making jobs, especially in smaller candy factories, are still done by hand.

In some plants, *candy makers* are responsible for many of the steps in production, including formulating recipes and mixing, cooking, and forming candy. *Candy-maker helpers* help candy makers by tending machines, mixing ingredients, washing equipment, and performing other tasks. In large plants these jobs are often performed by different workers, under the direction of *candy supervisors.* Plants also employ *factory helpers,* who move trays from machine to machine and help confectionery workers in other ways.

After candy is formed, it is packaged, usually by machine, and delivered to distributors and eventually to retail stores.

EXPLORING

- Visit Web sites that will teach you more about candy. Here are two suggestions: The Cocoa Tree (http://www. thecocoatree.com) and eHOW: Candy History (http://www. ehow.com/candy-history).
- Try making candy at home. Fudge, taffy, candied apples, and chocolate-covered pretzels are among the sweets you can make in your own kitchen.
- Is there a candy manufacturing plant in your area? Call to see if tours are available.

- If you are in high school, get a part-time or summer job at a candy store or the candy department of a large store where you can learn what products are popular, how the candy is stored and handled, and how to package it for customers.
- If there is a candy manufacturer in your area, you may be able to get part-time or summer work as a helper while you are still in high school.

Candy sales workers sell candy to retail stores or distributors. *Route drivers* deliver candy to customers.

Confectionery industry workers work for a variety of employers. Some work in small candy stores that make their own confections. Others work in corporations that have plants in more than one country.

Education and Training

A high school diploma usually is required for employment in the confectionery industry. After you are hired, you will learn production skills on the job. High school courses in chemistry, biology, and shop are useful as background for some jobs, but skills are gained only through experience. Family and consumer science classes may offer you the opportunity to learn about cooking, baking, and food products. For some advanced positions, such as candy maker, workers may need technical expertise in food chemistry or other fields, as well as a solid knowledge of the industry. People who want to work in sales should take business and marketing classes.

You will need a bachelor's degree with an emphasis in food science technology and business courses if you want to advance to management positions.

Earnings

Confectionery workers' wages vary widely depending on such factors as the workers' skills and the size and location of the plant. According to the U.S. Department of Labor, weekly earnings for sugar and confectionery production workers averaged $642 in 2008. This wage translates into a yearly income of approximately $33,384. Since this amount is the average, there are both workers making more than this salary and workers making less. Entry-level, unskilled workers, such as helpers, may earn little more than the minimum wage ($7.25 an hour), especially in smaller and nonunion factories. Those working full time at the federal hourly minimum pay rate would have annual incomes of approximately $15,080.

DID YOU KNOW?

- Four hundred companies manufacture more than 90 percent of confectionery and chocolate products in the United States.
- Although candy is produced in 35 states, the candy industry is most active in Pennsylvania, New Jersey, Illinois, California, New York, Wisconsin, Texas, Virginia, and Ohio.
- The industry employs approximately 65,000 workers.
- To create its products, the industry annually uses three billion pounds of sugar, 635 million pounds of milk or milk products, 322 million pounds of domestic peanuts, 43 million pounds of California almonds, and 1.7 billion pounds of corn syrup sweeteners.

Source: Chocolate Manufacturers Association

Tips for Success

To be a successful confectionery industry worker, you should

- have good manual dexterity
- be able to work as a member of a team
- be in good physical health
- be willing to continue to learn throughout your career
- have good communication skills

Outlook

Candy making has become increasingly automated. It is often possible to produce candy products from the raw materials to the finished, packaged product without that product having

FOR MORE INFO

For industry information, contact
American Association of Candy Technologists
711 West Water Street
PO Box 266
Princeton, WI 54968-9146
920-295-6969
aactcinfo@gomc.com
http://www.aactcandy.org

For a wealth of information about candy and the confectionery industry, contact
National Confectioners Association
1101 30th Street, NW, Suite 200
Washington, DC 20007-3769

202-534-1440
info@candyusa.com
http://www.candyusa.com

For industry information, contact
PMCA
2980 Linden Street, Suite E3
Bethlehem, PA 18017-3283
610-625-4655
info@pmca.com
http://www.pmca.com

ever been touched by human hands. As more and more confectionery producers use automated machinery and equipment, the need for production workers, especially unskilled workers who do not have a college education, will decrease. In addition, the trend toward company consolidations will likely continue, meaning fewer employers of confectionery workers. Employment is expected to decline for sales workers and managers.

Most new openings will arise as workers change jobs. Large wholesale confectionery companies will provide the most employment opportunities.

Cookbook and Recipe Writers

What Cookbook and Recipe Writers Do

Most of us love food. Some people like to cook food. And others like to write about food. *Cookbook writers* write cookbooks. They may work as staff writers for a book publisher or be self-employed. To write a cookbook, cookbook writers need to first decide what type of cookbook they would like to write. Do they want to write a general cookbook that covers every course in a meal (such as appetizers, salads, breads, soups, meats, vegetables, and desserts) or a cookbook that focuses on one ingredient (lobster, for example) or one course (such as soup)? Do they want to write a regional cookbook (about food from a particular region in the United States or world)? An ethnic cookbook (focusing on food from Italy, Japan, Mexico, or another culture)? Or an appliance- or equipment-related cookbook (focusing on cooking with a bread machine, microwave, or outdoor grill)?

Once they have decided what type of cookbook to write, cookbook writers develop the various sections of the book. They create a rough outline, which details the features (recipes, of course, but perhaps a glossary and other resources) that will be included in the book. Then they develop their recipe ideas. Recipes are a set of instructions that people use to prepare a food dish. They prepare each recipe many times to ensure that they have accurately presented measurements, portion sizes, ingredients, and any other component that may make or break a recipe. As they prepare the recipe, they take notes on the pro-

EXPLORING

- Read books about food and cooking.
- Visit recipe Web sites. Here are a few suggestions: KidsHealth: Recipes (http://kidshealth.org/kid/recipes), Recipe Source (http://www.recipesource.com), Food Network (http://www.foodnetwork.com), and MarthaStewart.com (http://www.marthastewart.com/food).
- Take cooking classes offered by your school or community organizations.
- Try writing and preparing your own recipes. Be sure to take notes as you prepare each dish to help you determine what went right and what went wrong.
- Ask your teacher or parent to arrange an information interview with a cookbook or recipe writer.

cess for later review. The recipe development process will be much easier if the cookbook writer is comfortable in the kitchen and familiar with cooking techniques.

As they create and test the recipes, cookbook writers may also begin working on the other sections in the book. This allows them to tie in all of the various segments of the book so that they make sense to the readers. The table of contents details the various sections in the book. The writer creates it by referring to the original outline. The introduction covers the focus of the book and, perhaps, the writer's personal reasons for writing the book. A how-to section gives the reader instructions on how to do a specific task, such as how to cut meat or dice vegetables. The glossary contains definitions of cooking-related terms, such as broil, blend, and baste. The bibliography lists other books and articles that the writer referred to as he or she wrote the book.

It takes many other publishing professionals to create a cookbook. *Food photographers* take pictures of food, cooking utensils and equipment, and any other food-related subject matter that will appear in the cookbook. Some cookbook writers may pursue training in photography and take their own photographs. *Food stylists* arrange the food to look as tasty and appealing as possible. *Food editors* ensure that text provided by food writers is suitable in content, format, and style for the intended audience. *Graphic designers* design and layout the book and create any food-oriented illustrations that appear in the book. They use computer software programs to design and layout publications or create Web sites.

Recipe writers create recipes for books, magazines, newspapers, Web sites, and any other publication or product that features food-related articles and recipes. Recipes typically have the following components: the name of the dish, the amount of time needed to prepare the dish, the ingredients (usually listed in the order that they will be used), the equipment (stove, microwave, blender, baking pans, etc.), an ordered list of preparation instructions, and the number of servings the recipe will make. Recipe writers may also include information about the region or culture from which the recipe originated, nutritional information (including calories, fat content, etc.), and potential variations (such as a low-fat or low-carb version of the recipe) or substitutions (such as using skim milk instead of whole milk) that the reader may use when preparing the dish.

To create a useful recipe, recipe writers should explain every step, ingredient, and preparation process in detail. This helps readers to prepare the recipe as easily as possible. They should also prepare their finished recipe many times to ensure that it contains no errors or confusing instructions.

Recipe writers also may work with food photographers, food stylists, food editors, and graphic designers. They work as freelance writers or as full-time employees at companies that publish recipes and related products.

Fame & Fortune: Rick Bayless

When chef Rick Bayless prepares Mexican food, don't expect just tacos and chimichangas. His idea of Mexican is traditional regional fare such as Oaxacan tamales and moles, or perhaps a Central Mexico-inspired menudo or pozole. In fact, Bayless is credited by many people in the food and restaurant industry for introducing authentic Mexican cuisine to Americans.

Coming from a family of restaurant owners and grocers, Bayless always had strong roots in food, especially dishes that were prepared with fresh ingredients. However, it was his college work in Spanish and Latin American studies, as well as time spent living in Mexico, that inspired his love of Mexican cuisine.

Currently, Bayless owns several restaurants specializing in contemporary regional Mexican cooking—Frontera Grill, and its fine-dining counterpart, Topolobampo, Frontera Fresco, and the newest, Xoco—serving Mexican street food and snacks. His innovative menus at Frontera Grill and Topolobampo have earned Bayless numerous awards.

Bayless has also brought his love for Mexican food to print, winning several awards for his cookbooks. His first cookbook, *Authentic Mexican: Regional Cooking from the Heart of Mexico,* is considered a classic. In 1997, another one of his books, *Rick Bayless's Mexican Kitchen: Capturing the Vibrant Flavors of a World-Class Cuisine,* was awarded "Cookbook of the Year" by the International Association of Culinary Professionals. He has also written several other books, including *Fiesta at Rick's: Fabulous Food for Great Times with Friends* and *Salsas That Cook: Using Classic Salsas To Enliven Our Favorite Dishes.*

Besides cooking and writing, Bayless founded the Frontera Farmer Foundation to help promote small sustainable farms in the Midwest area. This nonprofit organization benefits both farmers and restaurants. Using the group's capital development grants, farmers are able to start and sustain their farms, and grow a wide range of organic crops. Area restaurants and their patrons then have ready access to fresh local produce.

Bayless is also a noted television personality, hosting a PBS cooking show and competing in several Food Network cooking competitions. He is also a visiting staff member at the Culinary Institute of America. In recent years, his cooking skills were showcased at a White House State Dinner that honored the president of Mexico.

Source: Rickbayless.com

Tips for Success

To be a successful cookbook and recipe writer, you should

- have a passion for cooking
- be an expert in cooking and baking techniques and ingredients
- be an excellent writer
- enjoy helping people learn more about food
- be very organized
- be able to meet deadlines

Education and Training

If you are interested in becoming a cookbook and recipe writer, take English, general science, home economics, and computer classes while in high school. Writers must be expert communicators, so you should be very good in English. Working on your school's newspaper, yearbook, or any other publication in high school will be useful.

Most cookbook and recipe writing jobs require a college education. Typical majors include English, communications, or culinary arts. A few colleges offer majors or minors in food writing.

Some employers require you to earn a degree or certificate from culinary school, or culinary work experience, in addition to a background in writing. You may wish to take cooking classes from a local culinary school or community college to enhance your chances of landing a job.

Earnings

According to the International Association of Culinary Professionals, cookbook authors typically earn $5,000 to $10,000 for their first book. Cookbook and recipe writers who work on staff at a publication earn $19,000 to $40,000 annually. Freelance

FOR MORE INFO

The following organization's Web site provides information on issues facing food writers and editors:

Association of Food Journalists
7 Avenida Vista Grande, Suite B7, #467
Santa Fe, NM 87508-9207
505-466-4742
http://www.afjonline.com

This organization provides a wealth of industry information at its Web site.

International Association of Culinary Professionals
1100 Johnson Ferry Road, Suite 300
Atlanta, GA 30342-1733

404-252-3663
info@iacp.com
http://www.iacp.com

This organization offers an online newsletter and magazine at its Web site.

International Food, Wine & Travel Writers Association
1142 South Diamond Bar Boulevard, #177
Diamond Bar, CA 91765-2203
877-439-8929
admin@ifwtwa.org
http://www.ifwtwa.org

food writers earn $100 to $1,000 per story. Salaries are generally higher in large cities. Salaries also depend on the employer, as larger publishers tend to pay more, and the writer's level of experience. Those with many years of experience are able to earn a larger salary.

Outlook

There should be fair job opportunities for cookbook and recipe writers during the next decade. Although food-related publications are very popular, aspiring cookbook and recipe writers will have a tough time breaking into this fascinating field. However, cookbooks and other publications that feature recipes continue to grow in popularity. This growth means that there will be more opportunities for those who wish to pursue a career in food writing.

Cooking Instructors

EXPLORING

- Watch cooking shows on television.
- Take a cooking class to learn more about the field and to observe a cooking instructor at work. Many cooking schools offer classes for young people.
- Visit the Web sites of culinary schools to learn more about their educational programs. Visit http://www.acfchefs.org for a list of schools.
- Ask your teacher or parent to set up an information interview with a cooking instructor.
- If you are in high school, talk to your home economics teacher about his or her career.

What Cooking Instructors Do

Cooking instructors are teachers just like the ones you have at school. But instead of teaching social studies or physical education, they teach people how to cook. Students range from casual cooks who simply want to learn more about a specific cuisine (particular cooking practices and traditions) or improve their baking skills to people who want to cook as a career and work in the restaurant or food service industries. Cooking instructors teach students at culinary and technical schools; private adult education enterprises; community colleges; middle, junior high, and high schools; and in any other setting where the art of cooking is taught.

Typical courses in a college-level culinary education program include math; speech; economics; food history; food service; quantity food production; nutrition; food safety and sanitation; menu

A cooking instructor helps a student with her pie crust during class. (Jessica MacDonald, *Syracuse Newspapers*/The Image Works)

development; cost control; knife skills; purchasing; kitchen, employee, and restaurant management; computers in the food industry; ethics; wines and beverages; soups, stocks, and sauces; pastry; bread baking; meat identification and preparation; seafood identification and preparation; and foreign language (e.g., Spanish, French, or Italian). Other courses may educate students about regional, national, or international culinary styles and techniques. Some schools may offer classes that teach students how to write a resume or interview for a job.

Cooking instructors at the college-level spend about 80 percent of their class time conducting hands-on instruction with students in lab kitchens. Some postsecondary institutions even feature working restaurants where students can sharpen their culinary skills by preparing and serving food to actual customers. Instructors spend the rest of their class time demonstrating culinary techniques, lecturing students, assigning readings and homework, and taking attendance. Outside of class, they prepare and administer lessons and exams and grade student work. They also meet with students individually to discuss class progress and grades.

Cooking instructors at the middle, junior high, and high school levels typically are known as *home economics teachers*

Helping Hands: Chef & Child Foundation

Chefs don't just spend their time in the kitchen or on television cooking shows. Some try to make the world a better place. The American Culinary Federation (ACF) Education Foundation Chef & Child Foundation Inc. was founded in 1989 to help "educate children and families in understanding proper nutrition through community-based initiatives led by ACF chef members, and to be the voice of the culinary industry in its fight against childhood hunger, malnutrition and obesity."

The foundation provides grants to local communities, offers cooking classes for children in grades three through eight, provides fitness and nutrition activities for kids, and hosts National Nutrition Month every March.

Visit http://www.acfchefs.org to learn more about the foundation.

Source: American Culinary Federation

or *family and consumer science teachers.* They teach students about basic nutrition, food safety and sanitation, and cooking techniques.

Education and Training

To prepare for a career as a cooking instructor, take high school courses in family and consumer science, English, math, business, and science. Since many cooking terms are derived from the French language, you might want to take French. Other foreign languages that might be useful include Spanish and Italian.

Culinary arts institutions typically require teachers to have at least a bachelor's degree in culinary arts and at least three years experience in the restaurant or food service industries.

Earnings

Earnings vary widely according to the number of courses taught, the instructor's experience, and the area of the country where the institution is located. Salaries for all postsecondary teachers ranged from less than $31,000 to $129,000 or more in 2010, according to the U.S. Department of Labor. Self-enrichment education teachers had median annual earnings of $36,340 in 2010. Middle, junior high, and high school cooking instructors earn salaries that range from less than $37,000 to $80,000 or more annually.

DID YOU KNOW?

There are two main types of cooking: moist-heat cooking and dry-heat cooking. Following are some of the most popular ways to cook using moist or dry heat:

Moist-Heat Methods
- Boiling
- Braising
- Simmering
- Steaming

Dry-Heat Methods
- Baking
- Barbecuing
- Broiling/Grilling
- Frying
- Microwaving
- Roasting

FOR MORE INFO

For information on apprenticeships and culinary trends, contact
American Culinary Federation Inc.
180 Center Place Way
St. Augustine, FL 32095-8859
800-624-9458
acf@acfchefs.net
http://www.acfchefs.org

For information on educational programs, including classes for kids, contact
The Culinary Institute of America
1946 Campus Drive
Hyde Park, NY 12538-1430

845-452-9600
http://www.ciachef.edu

This organization provides a wealth of industry information at its Web site.
International Association of Culinary Professionals
1100 Johnson Ferry Road, Suite 300
Atlanta, GA 30342-1733
404-252-3663
info@iacp.com
http://www.iacp.com

Because many cooking instructors work part time, they are often paid by the hour or by the course, with no health insurance or other benefits. Hourly pay ranges from $6 to $50.

Outlook

An increasing number of people want to learn how to cook. Some just want to learn as a hobby, but many people want to train to become professional cooks and chefs. This is good news for aspiring cooking instructors who will be needed to teach students. Overall, employment for all postsecondary teachers is expected to be good during the next decade. Employment for middle, junior high, and high school teachers should also be steady.

Cooks and Chefs

What Cooks and Chefs Do

Who makes the food you eat at restaurants? *Cooks and chefs* do! Cooks and chefs prepare and cook food in restaurants, hotels, cafeterias, and other eating places. They plan menus, order food, and measure and mix ingredients. They also cook and test the food and arrange it on plates. Some specialize in a certain area, such as cutting meat, boning fish, fixing sauces, or making salads, soups, or desserts.

EXPLORING

- Practice cooking for your family and friends. Ask relatives for recipes and also keep an eye out for them in magazines and on prepared food boxes, or you can create your own recipes.
- Visit recipe Web sites. Here are a few suggestions: KidsHealth: Recipes (http://kidshealth.org/kid/recipes), Recipe Source (http://www.recipesource.com),
- Food Network (http://www.foodnetwork.com), and MarthaStewart.com (http://www.marthastewart.com/food).
- Help your mom or dad prepare a meal.
- Volunteer at a local kitchen that serves the homeless or others in need.
- Ask your teacher to set up a presentation by a cook or chef.

A chef puts the finishing touches on a dish. (Judi Bottoni, AP Photo)

Chefs may do many of these things, but their major job is to oversee all the activities in the kitchen. They also create recipes and train cooks. It is the responsibility of the chef to keep track of work schedules. Some chefs specialize in a particular cooking style, such as French or Italian.

Cooks and chefs may work a long week of 48 hours or more. (Most people only work 35 to 40 hours each week.) This usually includes evening and weekend work because that is when many people eat in restaurants.

Fame & Fortune: Julia Child

The famous chef Julia Child often credited her love for food, French in particular, to a dish she once ate in Rouen, France. That dish was, in part, her inspiration to learn how to cook properly. While her husband worked for the U.S. State Department in Paris, Child decided to fill her time by enrolling in the famous cooking school, Le Cordon Bleu. There she learned the proper techniques to cook French cuisine.

After graduation, Child began to teach French cooking classes to American women living in Paris. The classes, soon known as the School of the Three Food Lovers, were taught by Julia and her two close friends. It was this friendship that prompted the idea of writing a cookbook. This was no ordinary cookbook, but rather one that presented true French recipes that could easily be duplicated in everyday American kitchens. After many rejections and revisions, *Mastering the Art of French Cooking* was published in 1961. Still in print, the cookbook is regarded as a classic.

Child wrote many other cookbooks since *Mastering the Art of French Cooking,* but it was her television work that many people remember. In 1962, Child gave a demonstration on the proper way to cook an omelet, which was shown on a small Boston public broadcasting station. This was the start of the widely popular national show *The French Chef.* The show ran for 10 seasons and covered such topics as how to prepare capon (a young male chicken), master desserts such as soufflés, or season a cassoulet (a slow-cooked casserole or bean stew). The audiences followed her tips and recipes, but were attracted to her enthusiasm, charming personality, and quick wit. The show won several Peabody and Emmy Awards, and was the first television show captioned for the deaf. Child became the first woman to be inducted into the Culinary Institute Hall of Fame in 1993.

Julia Child died in 2004. Her studio kitchen is on display at the Smithsonian's National Museum of American History (http://americanhistory.si.edu/julia child). *Julie & Julia,* a movie about her life that starred Meryl Streep and Amy Adams, was released in 2009.

Sources: Biography.com, Smithsonian
National Museum of American History

Profile: Chef Marie-Antoine Carême (1784–1833)

Marie-Antoine Carême is often regarded as the "father of French haute cuisine" (high-quality cooking). Though he was born more than two hundred years ago, many of his innovations are still used in fine French cooking today.

Carême was the first to classify sauces—a cornerstone of many French dishes—according to their main ingredients: milk, brown stock, white stock, and egg yolk. Carême found that by changing a single ingredient, or combining them with others, there were many different preparation possibilities.

Carême also had a different approach to pastry. He gave his own interpretations to classic recipes such as sponge cakes and cream puff pastry, but also developed new recipes. The recipe for Charlotte russe—a pastry with whipped cream and gelatin can be attributed to Carême.

Carême also believed in the importance of food presentation. He loved to serve food in unexpected ways such as standing it on end, creating shapes, or using different garnishes and decorations. Luckily, Carême wrote down his recipes, many of which are still used today. He included many engraved illustrations in his cookbooks, a practice seldom found at the time.

Carême is also credited with creating the chef toque—the tall white hat associated with chefs.

Sources: Foodreference.com, Enotes.com

Successful cooks and chefs have a keen interest in food preparation and cooking. They like to experiment to develop new recipes and new food combinations. They should be able to work as part of a team and to work under pressure during rush hours, in close quarters, and with a certain amount of noise and confusion. These employees need an even temperament and patience to interact with the public daily and to work closely with many other kinds of employees.

Although cooks and chefs sometimes also bake, *bakers* specialize in preparing only baked goods, such as cakes, pastries, cookies, rolls, muffins, biscuits, breads, and other treats. These are sold at bakeries, hotels, restaurants, cafeterias, and large food-chain stores.

Personal chefs prepare menus for individuals and their families. They purchase the ingredients for the meals, then cook, package, and store the meals in the clients' own kitchens. Personal chefs typically own their own businesses.

Education and Training

Some cooks and chefs enter the profession through on-the-job training in restaurants or hotels. Although a high school diploma is not always required, it is essential for those who wish to move up to better jobs. In high school, you can prepare for a career as a cook or chef by taking classes in family and consumer science. Since many cooking terms are derived from the French language, courses in French and other languages should also be helpful.

The best job opportunities are available to those who graduate from a special cooking school or culinary institute. These schools offer classes in menu planning, food costs, purchasing, food storage, sanitation, health standards, and cooking and baking techniques. Graduates may have to serve as an apprentice or work in a supporting role before being hired as a head chef in a top restaurant or hotel.

Earnings

Salaries for cooks and chefs vary widely based on many factors, such as the size, type, and location of the establishment, and the skill, experience, training, and specialization of the worker. Chefs and head cooks had median earnings of $40,630 in 2010, according to the U.S. Department of Labor. Salaries ranged from less than $24,000 to $70,000 or more. Full-service restau-

FOR MORE INFO

For information on training, contact
AIB International
PO Box 3999
Manhattan, KS 66505-3999
785-537-4750
http://www.aibonline.org

For information on apprenticeships and culinary trends, contact
American Culinary Federation Inc.
180 Center Place Way
St. Augustine, FL 32095-8859
800-624-9458
acf@acfchefs.net
http://www.acfchefs.org

For information on culinary education, contact
American Hotel and Lodging Educational Institute
800 North Magnolia Avenue, Suite 1800
Orlando, FL 32803-3271
800-752-4567
http://www.ahlei.org

For information on a career as a personal chef, contact
American Personal & Private Chef Association
4572 Delaware Street
San Diego, CA 92116-1005
800-644-8389
info@personalchef.com
http://www.personalchef.com

For information on educational programs, including classes for kids, contact
The Culinary Institute of America
1946 Campus Drive
Hyde Park, NY 12538-1430

845-452-9600
http://www.ciachef.edu

This organization provides a wealth of industry information at its Web site.
International Association of Culinary Professionals
1100 Johnson Ferry Road, Suite 300
Atlanta, GA 30342-1733
404-252-3663
info@iacp.com
http://www.iacp.com

For information on education and careers, contact
National Restaurant Association Educational Foundation
175 West Jackson Boulevard, Suite 1500
Chicago, IL 60604-2702
800-765-2122
http://www.nraef.org

For information about a career as a research chef, contact
Research Chefs Association
1100 Johnson Ferry Road, Suite 300
Atlanta, GA 30342-1733
404-252-3663
rca@kellencompany.com
http://www.culinology.com

The USPCA offers training courses and mentorship opportunities.
United States Personal Chef Association (USPCA)
5728 Major Boulevard, Suite 750
Orlando, FL 32819-7963
800-995-2138
http://www.uspca.com

rant cooks had mean earnings of $42,420, and cooks working at institutions or cafeterias earned $22,730 a year. Cooks at fast food restaurants were at the bottom of the pay scale, earning $18,100 per year. Cooks and chefs usually receive their meals free during working hours and are furnished with any necessary job uniforms.

Outlook

Overall, good employment opportunities are expected for cooks and chefs during the next decade. Some careers, such as fast food cooks, may not see much growth in the number of new jobs because new, advanced machines require fewer people to operate them. However, many people leave this career for other jobs, and the need to find replacement cooks and chefs will mean many job opportunities in all areas. The need for cooks and chefs will also grow as the population increases and lifestyles change. As people make more money and have more leisure time, they eat out more often and take more vacations. In addition, working parents and their families dine out frequently as a convenience. Cooks and chefs with an educational background in business will have the best prospects—especially at restaurant chains. More companies are trying to save money by better managing expenses, and cooks and chefs who are able to work well with money and budgets will be in demand.

Dietitians and Nutritionists

What Dietitians and Nutritionists Do

Your mom and dad are probably always telling you what to eat (fruits and vegetables) and what not to eat (hot dogs, cheeseburgers, and ice cream). They are not just trying to bug you, but keep you healthy and strong. Too many hot dogs and ice cream cones can make you sick and overweight. Your parents aren't the only ones who give advice on nutrition. Did you know that there are professionals who advise people on eating habits and plan diets that will improve or maintain their health? They are known as *dietitians* and *nutritionists.* They work for themselves or for institutions such as hospitals, schools, restaurants, and hotels.

Registered dietitians (RDs) have completed strict training and testing requirements designed by the American Dietetic Association. They have a broad-based knowledge of foods, dietetics, and food service. They work in many settings.

Clinical dietitians plan and supervise the preparation of diets designed for patients. They work for hospitals and retirement homes. In many cases, patients cannot eat certain foods for medical reasons, such as diabetes or liver failure. Dietitians see that these patients receive nourishing meals. They work closely with doctors, who advise them regarding their patients' health and the foods that the patients cannot eat.

Community dietitians usually work for clinics, government health programs, social service agencies, or similar organizations. They counsel individuals or advise the members of cer-

EXPLORING

- Learn about the Food Pyramid by visiting http://www.my-pyramid.gov.
- Visit the following Web sites to learn more about opportunities in the field: American Dietetic Association: It's About Eating Right (http://www.eatright.org/Public) and ExploreHealthCareers.org (http://explorehealthcareers.org).
- Read books about healthy diet and nutrition. Many cookbooks that feature healthy recipes have sections on nutrition.
- Learn healthy ways to cook and bake. Plan and prepare meals for your family. Do your own grocery shopping, and learn to pick out the best produce, meats, fish, and other ingredients. Take cooking classes offered by your school and other organizations in your community.
- Ask a teacher or counselor to arrange an information interview with a dietitian or nutritionist.

tain groups about nutritional problems, proper eating, and sensible grocery shopping.

Certified clinical nutritionists have the same core educational and internship backgrounds as RDs but are specialists who have completed some postgraduate education that focuses on the biochemical and physiological aspects of nutrition science. Certified clinical nutritionists typically work in private practice for themselves, as part of a group of health care professionals, or for a doctor or doctors in private practice. They work with clients to correct imbalances in the clients' biochemistry and improve their physiological function.

A school dietitian teaches a third-grade class about good nutrition. (Suzanne Carr-Rossi, AP Photo/*The Free Lance-Star*)

Although most dietitians and nutritionists do some kind of teaching in the course of their work, *teaching dietitians and nutritionists* specialize in education. They usually work for hospitals. They may teach full time or part time. Sometimes, teaching dietitians and nutritionists also perform other tasks. For example, they may run a food service operation, especially at small colleges.

Consultant dietitians and nutritionists work with schools, restaurants, grocery-store chains, manufacturers of food-

Profile: Antoine-Laurent Lavoisier (1743–1794)

Antoine-Laurent Lavoisier was a French chemist who is known as the "father of nutrition and chemistry" for his work in these fields.

Lavoisier was born in 1743. As he grew into young adulthood, his father, a successful lawyer, wanted him to follow in his footsteps and practice law. Lavoisier obtained his law license, but soon realized that he was more interested in studying science—particularly geology. He also studied astronomy and botany and wrote an award-winning essay on how to light the dark streets of a big city at night. At the age of 25, Lavoisier was elected to the Royal Academy of Science.

Lavoisier began to study the way the body uses food energy, or calories. He also studied the relationship between heat production and the use of energy and the composition of air, among other studies.

Lavoisier had a strong interest in politics and social justice. His ideas and beliefs would be the cause of his downfall during the French Revolution. Based on false charges, he was arrested, tried, and executed.

Sources: Chemical Heritage Foundation, Creighton University, Antoine-lavoisier.com

service equipment, drug companies, and private companies of various kinds. Some consultants work with athletes and sports teams. They help improve athletes' performance and extend the length of their careers.

Research dietitians and nutritionists work for government organizations, universities, hospitals, drug companies, and manufacturers. They try to improve existing food products or find alternatives to unhealthy foods.

Education and Training

Recommended high school courses for those who want to become dietitians and nutritionists include biology, chemistry,

Tips for Success

To be a successful dietitian or nutritionist, you should

- be detail oriented
- enjoy math and science
- be able to work as a member of a team
- have good communication skills
- enjoy helping people live healthier lives
- be willing to continue to learn throughout your career

health, family and consumer science, math, and communications.

To become a registered dietitian, you must have a bachelor's degree in dietetics, food service systems management, foods and nutrition, or a related area. There are no specific educational requirements for nutritionists who are not dietitians, but most nutritionists have at least two years of college-level training in nutrition, food service, or another related subject. Many employers require nutritionists to have a bachelor's degree. If you want to teach, do research, or work in the field of public health, you will need one or more advanced degrees.

Earnings

Dietitians and nutritionists earned median annual salaries of $53,250 in 2010, according to the U.S. Department of Labor. New workers earned less than $34,000. Very experienced dietitians and nutritionists earned more than $75,000. Dietitians and nutritionists who were employed at hospitals earned mean annual salaries of about $54,000.

Outlook

Employment of dietitians and nutritionists is expected to be good during the next decade. People are becoming more aware of the importance of nutrition, and they are asking experts for advice. The average age of the population is increasing. This will create a demand for nutritional counseling and planning

FOR MORE INFO

The ADA is the single best source of information about careers in dietetics. Visit its Web site for educational and career information.

American Dietetic Association (ADA)
120 South Riverside Plaza, Suite 2000
Chicago, IL 60606-6995
800-877-1600
http://www.eatright.org

The goal of the ASN is to improve peoples' quality of life through the nutritional sciences.

American Society for Nutrition (ASN)
9650 Rockville Pike
Bethesda, MD 20814-3999

301-634-7050
info@asns.org
http://www.nutrition.org

For information on certification, contact
International and American Associations of Clinical Nutritionists
15280 Addison Road, Suite 130
Addison, TX 75001-4551
972-407-9089
ddc@clinicalnutrition.com
http://www.iaacn.org

in schools, residential care facilities, prisons, community health programs, and home health care agencies. Opportunities for dietitians will be best in contract providers of food services (outside companies that provide food services to organizations), in offices of physicians and other health practitioners, and in outpatient care centers. Hospital and nursing home dietitians may experience slower employment growth or even decline. Many hospitals and nursing homes are expected to hire outside companies to handle food-service operations.

Dietitians and nutritionists with advanced training and certification will have the best employment opportunities. Those with less than a bachelor's degree will have a tough time landing a job.

Family and Consumer Scientists

What Family and Consumer Scientists Do

Family and consumer scientists are concerned with the well-being of the home and family. They work in education, dietetics, research, social welfare, extension services, business, and in other settings. Whatever the job, family and consumer scientists rely on their understanding of food and nutrition, child development, household management, and the many other elements involved in day-to-day living.

Family and consumer scientists who work as teachers in junior and senior high schools teach courses such as nutrition, sewing, cooking, child development, family relations, and home management. Teachers at the college level prepare students for careers in home economics. They also conduct research and write articles and textbooks.

Extension-service family and consumer scientists are part of an educational system supported by government agencies to educate and advise families, both rural and urban. They teach these families about nutrition, child care, and other aspects of homemaking. These scientists offer help and advice over the phone and may also travel to various communities to give presentations and assistance.

Health and welfare agencies hire family and consumer scientists to work with social workers, nurses, and physicians. They give advice to low-income families who need help with financial

EXPLORING

- Take home economics classes. These will teach you the basics of cooking, sewing, and home management.
- Use your library and Internet resources to learn all you can about areas of family and consumer science that interest you, such as nutrition, child care, or consumer trends.
- Your community 4-H club may offer opportunities in community service, arts, consumer and family sciences, environmental education, and healthy lifestyle education. Visit http://4-h.org for more information.
- Talk to a family and consumer scientist about his or her career.

management concerns. They develop community programs in health and nutrition, money management, and child care.

The business world offers many opportunities to family and consumer scientists. Some work for manufacturers, where they test and improve products and recipes and prepare booklets on uses of products. They plan educational programs and materials.

Family and consumer scientists who work in media and advertising agencies write about food, fashion, home decorations, budgets, and home management. Those who work for retail stores help customers choose furniture and other household items and also work in advertising, buying, and merchandising (presenting products in ways that make people want to buy them).

Some family and consumer scientists specialize in dietetics. They plan meals, order food and supervise its preparation, handle budgets, and plan special diets. They work in hospitals, hotels, restaurants, or schools.

Family and consumer scientists who work as *researchers* create products and develop procedures that make life better for families. Researchers work for colleges and universities, government and private agencies, and private companies.

Education and Training

In high school, take courses in English, math, foreign language, and history. You should also take any classes related to home economics, including child development, adult living, and health.

You will need at least a bachelor's degree in family and consumer science or home economics to work in this field. Many colleges and universities offer these degrees, as well as specialization in subjects such as education, child development, foods and nutrition, dietetics, institution management, textiles and clothing, family economics and home management, household equipment and furnishings, and applied art. Those who conduct research and teach college usually need a master's degree or a doctorate.

Earnings

Earnings among family and consumer scientists vary a great deal, depending on experience, education, and area of work. Those in entry-level positions, such

DID YOU KNOW?

Where Family and Consumer Scientists Work

- Adult education programs
- Colleges and universities
- Elementary schools
- Food and appliance manufacturers
- High schools
- Hospitals
- Hotels

Typical College Courses

- Apparel Merchandising
- Apparel Production
- Basic Nutrition
- Child Development
- Consumer Economics
- Family Financial Management
-

- Food Science
- Human Development
- Marriage and the Family
- Meal Management
- Nutrition in the Life Cycle

Source: CollegeBoard.com

as salespeople and child-care workers, may have annual earnings of well below $20,000. But teachers and those in upper-level sales and marketing jobs can earn considerably more. The U.S. Department of Labor reports the following median salaries for teachers in 2010 by educational level: elementary, $51,660; middle, $51,960; and secondary, $53,230. College home economics teachers had median annual earnings of $65,040 in 2010, according to the U.S. Department of Labor. Food scientists earned an average of $60,180 a year in 2010.

Outlook

The demand for family and consumer scientists will be highest for specialists in marketing, merchandising, family and consumer resource management, food service and institutional management, food science

FOR MORE INFO

For information on careers, contact
American Association of Family and Consumer Sciences
400 North Columbus Street, Suite 202
Alexandria, VA 22314-2264
800-424-8080
staff@aafcs.org
http://www.aafcs.org

and human nutrition, environment and shelter, and textiles and clothing. Also, with the elderly population growing, family and consumer scientists will be actively involved in social services, gerontology, home health care, adult day care services, and other programs that improve the quality of life for older people.

Those interested in teaching will find more opportunities at the elementary and secondary level than at the college level. Vocational education programs, youth pregnancy prevention, and at-risk youth are priorities for teachers and administrators.

Farmers

What Farmers Do

The food we eat doesn't grow by magic. It takes skilled workers called *farmers* to grow our food from seed to harvested plant, or raise the animals we eat. Farmers grow crops, such as peanuts, corn, wheat, cotton, fruits, or vegetables. They also raise cattle, pigs, sheep, chickens, and turkeys for food and keep herds of dairy cattle for milk. Throughout the early history of the United States, farming was a family affair. Today, however, family farms are disappearing. Most large farms are now run by agricultural corporations.

Farmers need good soil and a lot of water for their crops and animals. They need to know how to bring water to their plants (irrigation) and add rich nutrients (fertilizer) to the soil. They also need to know how to keep their animals and crops healthy. They must control insects and diseases that will damage or destroy crops or livestock. They also must provide proper care for farm animals (livestock), such as clean, warm shelters, proper food, and special breeding programs.

There are many types of specialized farmers. The following paragraphs detail a few of these specialties.

Livestock farmers buy calves from ranchers who breed and raise them. They feed and fatten young cattle and often raise their own corn and hay to lower feeding costs. They need to be familiar with cattle diseases and proper methods of feeding.

EXPLORING

- Read books and visit Web sites about farming.
- Once you are in high school, try to land a summer job as a farmhand.
- If you are between the ages of five and 22, you might also want to join the National Junior Horticulture Association, which offers horticulture-related projects, contests, and other activities, as well as career information. Visit http://www.njha.org for more information.
- Join other youth farming organizations such as 4-H and National FFA Organization.
- Talk to a farmer about his or her career.

They provide their cattle with fenced places to live (pasturage) and adequate shelter from rough weather.

Sheep ranchers raise sheep primarily for their wool, but also for meat. Large herds are maintained on rangeland in the western states.

Dairy farmers are mostly concerned with producing high-grade milk, but they also raise corn and grain to feed their animals. Dairy animals must be milked twice each day. Farmers clean stalls and barns by washing, sweeping, and sterilizing milking equipment with boiling water.

Poultry farmers usually do not hatch their own chicks but buy them from commercial hatcheries. The primary duty of poultry farmers is to keep their flocks healthy. They provide shelter from the chickens' natural enemies and from extreme weather conditions. The shelters are kept extremely clean, because diseases can spread through a flock rapidly. Some poultry farmers raise chickens to be sold as broilers or fryers. Others specialize in the production of eggs.

Tips for Success

To be a successful farmer, you should

- be an expert in farming methods
- enjoy working outdoors
- be willing to work long hours, including on weekends
- be a hard worker
- be organized
- have good business skills
- have mechanical ability
- be willing to continue to learn throughout your career

Beekeepers set up and manage beehives. They harvest and sell honey and also cultivate (raise) bees for lease to farmers to help pollinate (fertilize) their crops.

Aquaculture farmers raise fish, shellfish, or other aquatic life (such as aquatic plants) under controlled conditions for profit and/or human consumption. They are also known as *aquaculturists, fish farmers, fish culturists,* and *mariculturists.*

Organic farmers don't raise a certain type of crop or livestock. Instead they use environmentally friendly practices to grow crops or raise livestock. Example of this farming approach include limiting or not using chemicals on farm fields and allowing livestock to roam free on farmland instead of being confined to a small space (which may create healthier animals).

Education and Training

Courses in math and science, especially chemistry, statistics, business, earth science, and botany, are important. Accounting, bookkeeping, and computer courses are also very helpful.

After high school, you should enroll in either a two-year or a four-year course of study in a college of agriculture. For a person with no farm experience, a bachelor's degree in agriculture is essential. Many students earn a degree in business with a

Mmmm Good!

What do livestock eat? Animals need basic nutrients, such as proteins, carbohydrates, fats, minerals, and vitamins. Specially prepared feeds and roughage, such as hay, supply farm animals with these nutrients. Here's what goes into animal feeds:

- Pasturage (growing grasses, alfalfa, clover)
- Grains
- Hay
- Silage (pasturage and grains stored in airtight structures called silos and allowed to ferment)
- High-protein concentrates (soybean meal, cottonseed oil, blood meal, and bone meal)
- High-carbohydrate concentrates (corn, sorghum, molasses, and dehydrated potatoes)
- Food additives (hormones, antibiotics, vitamins, and minerals)
- Byproducts from packing-houses, fruit and vegetable processing plants, breweries, distilleries, and paper mills

concentration in agriculture, agricultural economics and business, animal science, agronomy, crop and fruit science, dairy science, farm management, or horticulture.

Some universities offer advanced studies in horticulture, animal science, agronomy, and agricultural economics. Most students in agricultural colleges also take courses in farm management, business, finance, and economics.

Earnings

Farmers' incomes change from year to year depending on weather, the condition of their farm machinery, the demand for their crops and livestock, and the costs of feed, land, and equipment. According to the U.S. Department of Labor, farm manag-

FOR MORE INFO

For information on beekeeping, contact
American Beekeeping Federation
3525 Piedmont Road, Building 5, Suite 300
Atlanta, GA 30305-1578
404-760-2875
info@abfnet.org
http://www.abfnet.org

The Farm Bureau hosts youth conferences
and other events for those interested in
farming.
American Farm Bureau Federation
600 Maryland Avenue, SW, Suite 1000W
Washington, DC 20024-2555
202-406-3600
http://www.fb.org

For industry information, contact
**American Society of Farm Managers and
Rural Appraisers**
950 South Cherry Street, Suite 508
Denver, CO 80246-2664
303-758-3513
http://www.asfmra.org

Organizations such as 4-H and the
National FFA Organization (formerly
Future Farmers of America) offer good
opportunities for learning about, visiting,
and participating in farming activities.

4-H Clubs
7100 Connecticut Avenue
Chevy Chase, MD 20815-4934
301-961-2800
info@fourhcouncil.edu
http://www.4h-usa.org

National FFA Organization
6060 FFA Drive
PO Box 68960
Indianapolis, IN 46268-0960
317-802-6060
http://www.ffa.org

For information on farm policies, education, and other news relating to the agricultural industry, visit the USDA Web site.
U.S. Department of Agriculture (USDA)
1400 Independence Avenue, SW
Washington, DC 20250-0002
202-720-2791
http://www.usda.gov

For information about aquaculture,
contact
World Aquaculture Society
143 J. M. Parker Coliseum
Louisiana State University
Baton Rouge, LA 70803-0001
225-578-3137
https://www.was.org

ers had median annual earnings of $40,640 in 2010. Earnings
ranged from less than $30,000 to $106,000 or more. Most farmers, especially those running small farms, earn incomes from
nonfarm activities that may be several times larger than their
farm incomes.

Outlook

Because farming is such a risky business, those entering the career cannot make it without family support or financial aid from banks or the government. Reports show that the number of farmers and farm laborers is decreasing. Rising costs and the trend toward larger farms are forcing out small farmers. Some farmers who operate specialty farms will have better job prospects. These include organic farmers and those who grow crops that are used in landscaping, such as shrubs, trees, and turf.

Despite the great difficulty in becoming a farmer today, there are many agriculture-related careers that involve people with farm production, marketing, management, and agribusiness.

Fishers

What Fishers Do

Fishers catch fish and other sea life and sell it to restaurants, fish markets, and other businesses. The various kinds of fishers are grouped according to the type of equipment they use, the type of fish they catch, and where they catch the fish.

Some fishers work alone in small boats and some work in crews of as many as 25 people or more in a fishing fleet. They can remain at sea for several days or for months at a time. Most commercial fishing is done in ocean waters far from home port. Only a small percentage of fish are caught in rivers, streams, ponds, or lakes, or harvested from fish farms.

Fishers who catch fish with nets are called *net fishers*. They make up the largest group of fishers. They catch most of the world's supply of fish. Net fishers use three main types of nets: seines, trawls, and gill nets.

EXPLORING

- Look for opportunities to go out on a fishing boat.
- Contact a state department of fish and game to learn more about the local fishing industry.
- If you don't live near the water, you can learn about saltwater fish by working for a pet shop or a state aquarium.
- Working at a fish market can acquaint you with different kinds of fish and consumer demand for seafood.
- Ask a school counselor to arrange an information interview with a fisher.

Fishers pull in a net of fish at a fish farm. (RIA Novosti/TopFoto/The Image Works)

Fishing crews use seines to catch schools of herring, mackerel, sardines, tuna, and other fish that swim near the surface of the ocean. In funnel-shaped nets called trawls, fishers catch shrimp, scallops, and other shellfish living on or near the ocean floor. Before they drop these nets, they use sonar to find where the greatest number of fish are located. Only a small number of fishers use the third type of net, the gill net. This net, which acts like a wall, entangles fish such as salmon, sharks, and herring.

Line fishers catch fish with poles, hooks, and lines. This takes a very long time. They work alone or in crews. They lay out lines and attach hooks, bait, and other equipment, depending on the type of fish they plan to catch. They then lower these lines into the water. To haul catches on board they use reels, winches, or their bare hands.

Tips for Success

To be a successful fisher, you should

- enjoy working as part of a team, but also independently when necessary
- be in excellent physical shape
- be willing to work long hours

- be able to stay calm in stressful situations
- be willing to be away from home for days or weeks at a time
- have mechanical skills
- have good business skills (if you own your own boat)

Pot fishers trap crab, lobster, and eel in cages containing bait. Some chase turtles and certain kinds of fish into net traps. They fish near the shore or in inland waters off small boats. Pot fishing is done by lowering the cages into the water, pulling them in when the fish is trapped, and dumping the catch onto the deck. Pot fishers often sell their catches live to processors who can freeze or sell them fresh.

Some fishers are primarily involved with recreational fishing. They operate fishing vessels for sport fishing, socializing, and relaxation.

All commercial fishers put in long hours and work under dangerous and difficult conditions. The work is exhausting. They must work in all kinds of weather. Sometimes they spend months at sea with the same group of people in cramped living conditions.

Education and Training

Generally, fishers learn their trade on the job. But some high schools, colleges, and technical schools offer courses in handling boats, fishing equipment, navigation, and meteorology. These provide good preparation for a job in fishing. Short-term

DID YOU KNOW?

- Fishers hold approximately 35,600 jobs in the United States.
- More than 50 percent of fishers are self-employed—one of the highest percentages of all careers in the United States.
- The majority of fishing takes place off Alaska, the Gulf Coast, Virginia, California, and New England.

Source: U.S. Department of Labor

courses offered by postsecondary schools provide information on electronic navigation and communications equipment and the latest improvements in fishing gear.

Earnings

The income of commercial fishers varies widely. It changes according to the seasons, the amount of fish available, what people want to buy, and the skills and dedication of the fisher. Usually, fishers cannot count on a fixed salary. Instead, they earn a percentage of the catch or an hourly wage. But they can increase their earnings by working faster, improving their skills, and learning all they can about the fishing industry. In New England, ship owners can receive 50 percent of the catch's receipts. The captain may receive 10 percent, and the captain and crew share the remaining 40 percent. According to the Alaska Department of Fish and Game, a crew member receiving 6 to 15 percent of the net profit, can earn between nothing and tens of thousands of dollars a year. According to the U.S. Department of Labor, fishers earned salaries that ranged from less than $17,000 to $40,000 or more in 2010.

Outlook

The fishing industry has experienced hard times in the past few decades. As a result, employment for fishers is expected to decline over the next several years. The industry is affected by environmental law, ship maintenance costs, improvements in electronic and other fishing gear (which has limited the expansion in crew size), and the increasing use of "floating processors," which process catches on-board, further limiting employ-

FOR MORE INFO

Visit the Alaska Department of Fish and Game Web site to learn more about commercial fishing, harvest statistics, and commercial fishing seasons.

Alaska Department of Fish and Game
Division of Commercial Fisheries
1255 West 8th Street
PO Box 115525
Juneau, AK 99811-5526
907-465-4100
http://www.cf.adfg.state.ak.us

The goals of the NMFS include building and maintaining sustainable fisheries. Visit its Web site for news and to sign up for the e-mail newsletter *FishNews.*

National Marine Fisheries Service (NMFS)
Partnerships & Communications
1315 East West Highway
Silver Spring, MD 20910-3282
http://www.nmfs.noaa.gov

This agency conducts research and provides information on the global oceans, atmosphere, space, and sun. It oversees the NMFS. Visit the NOAA Web site for news, statistics, and other information relating to fisheries.

National Oceanic and Atmospheric Administration (NOAA)
1401 Constitution Avenue, NW, Room 5128
Washington, DC 20230-0001
outreach@noaa.gov
http://www.noaa.gov

ment opportunities. However, new technology also helps the industry. For example, super-chilled refrigerator hulls help keep fish fresh for higher selling prices. Color monitors help fishers see the nets and fish while still under water.

Pollution and excessive fishing have decreased the fish stock, particularly in the North Atlantic and Pacific Northwest. Some states have limited the number of fishing permits to allow regrowth of fish and shellfish populations.

Food Service Workers

What Food Service Workers Do

Food service workers keep kitchens and dishes clean and help cooks make food. *Waiters, servers,* and *lunchroom or coffee shop counter attendants* take customers' orders, serve food and beverages, calculate bills, and collect money. Between serving customers, they clear and clean tables and counters, replenish supplies, and set up table service for future customers.

Some food service workers assist with food preparation. They gather the food and utensils and set up the pots and pans and other cooking equipment. They wash fruits and vegetables and chop ingredients for salads, sandwiches, or vegetable dishes. They mix ingredients, make coffee and tea, cook french fries, and do other tasks according to the cook's instructions.

Counter attendants also do some simple cooking tasks. These include making sandwiches, salads, and cold drinks and preparing ice cream dishes. They take customers' orders, fill them, and take payment at a cash register. They also may have to help clean kitchen equipment, sweep and mop floors, and carry out trash.

Waiters in full-service restaurants seat customers, present menus, suggest choices from the menu, and inform the customers of special preparations and seasonings of food. They take care of special requests and check each order to make sure it is correct before bringing it to the table.

Dining room attendants, also known as *waiters' assistants, buspersons,* or *bussers,* clear and reset tables, carry dirty dishes

EXPLORING

- Take cooking classes, and practice cooking for and serving your family.
- Volunteer for food service jobs with community centers, shelters, and social service agencies that serve meals to the needy.
- Get a part-time or summer job as a dining room attendant, counter worker, or waiter at a restaurant, grill, or coffee shop with a casual atmosphere.
- Dealing with the public is a large aspect of food service work, so get experience in this area. If you can't find employment in food service, look for work as a store clerk, cashier, or customer service worker.
- Talk to a food service worker about his or her career.

to the dishwashing area, carry in trays of food, and clean up spilled food and broken dishes. In some restaurants, these attendants also serve water and bread and butter to customers. They fill salt and pepper shakers, clean coffeepots, and do various other tasks.

Other food service workers scrape plates and load dishes in a dishwasher or wash them by hand. They clean the kitchen worktables, stoves, pots and pans, and other equipment. They sweep and mop the kitchen floor and throw away garbage. These workers are known as *kitchen assistants.*

Education and Training

You do not need to obtain any special education or training to work in an entry-level food service position. Training

A waitress at an outdoor café serves customers. (Oberhaeuser/Caro/The Image Works)

takes place on the job, so it is not always necessary to finish high school. However, classes in family and consumer science, cooking, math, and science are helpful. Food servers with experience can find better positions and higher tips at fine dining establishments. Some vocational schools offer special training courses for waiters.

If you are interested in owning or managing a restaurant, a high school diploma and additional education at a two- or four-year college of hotel or restaurant management is recommended.

Tips for Success

To be a successful food service worker, you should

- be in good physical condition
- be able to follow instructions
- have good communication skills

- be clean and properly dressed
- be able to work well as a member of a team
- have a pleasant personality

Earnings

Food service workers' earnings are determined by a number of factors, such as the type, size, and location of the food establishment, union membership, experience and training, basic wages, and in some cases, tips earned. Estimating the average wage scale therefore is difficult.

Most waiters depend on tips to supplement their hourly wages, which in general are relatively small. According to the U.S. Department of Labor, waiters and waitresses earned an average of $18,330 annually in 2010, including tips; full-time dining room attendants earned an average annual salary of $18,190. Food counter workers earned median annual salaries of $18,370, and dishwashers earned $18,150. Most businesses offer free or discounted meals to workers.

DID YOU KNOW?

- In 2008, 21 percent of food service workers were between the ages of 16 and 19.
- Approximately 7.7 million food service workers are employed in the United States.
- About 761,000 new food service jobs are expected to be available by 2018.

Source: U.S. Department of Labor

Outlook

Food service careers offer full-time and part-time, long-term and short-term

FOR MORE INFO

For information on accredited education programs, contact

International Council on Hotel, Restaurant, and Institutional Education
2810 North Parham, Suite 230
Richmond, VA 23294-4422
804-346-4800
http://www.chrie.org

For information on education and careers, contact

National Restaurant Association Educational Foundation
175 West Jackson Boulevard, Suite 1500
Chicago, IL 60604-2702

800-765-2122
http://www.nraef.org

For information on career opportunities in Canada, contact

Canadian Restaurant and Foodservices Association
316 Bloor Street West
Toronto, ON M5S 1W5 Canada
800-387-5649
info@crfa.ca
http://www.crfa.ca

opportunities for both skilled and unskilled people. They are a great option for students, parents of small children, seniors, people with disabilities, and people who are in between jobs.

Opportunities should be excellent for food service workers during the next decade. Many job openings will come from the need to replace workers who have left the field. Turnover is high in these jobs because of the low pay, the long hours, and the large number of students and others who do this work on a temporary basis before moving on to other occupations.

Food Technologists

What Food Technologists Do

Food technologists are scientists who study the ways that foods are processed, preserved, and packaged. They look for ways to improve the flavor, appearance, nutritional value, and convenience of food products. They also perform tests to make sure that products meet quality standards.

Food technologists usually specialize in one phase of the food industry. Food technologists in basic research study the physical and chemical composition of foods and observe the changes that take place during storage or processing. This research helps them understand what factors affect the flavor, appearance, or texture of foods. Other technologists create new food products and develop new processing methods. They may also work with existing foods to make them more nutritious and flavorful and to improve their color and texture.

A rapidly growing area of food technology is biotechnology. Food technologists in this area work with plant breeding, gene splicing, microbial fermentation, and plant cell tissue cultures to produce enhanced raw products for processing.

Food technologists conduct chemical tests on products to be sure they meet standards set by the government and by the food industry. They also determine the nutritive content (amounts of sugar, starch, protein, fat, vitamins, and minerals) in the product so that this information may be printed on the labels.

Some food technologists work in quality-control laboratories, where they focus on making sure that foods in every stage

EXPLORING

- Visit the following Web site for information and activities that explore the science behind cooking: The Accidental Scientist: The Science of Cooking (http://www.exploratorium.edu/cooking).
- Develop your interests in cooking, and experiment with inventing your own recipes.
-

- Chemistry is an important part of food technology, so participate in science clubs that allow you to explore chemical processes.
- Tour local food processing plants to see how food is produced and packaged on a large scale.
- Talk with a food technologist about his or her career.

of processing meet industry and government standards. They check to see that raw ingredients are fresh and suitable for processing. They also test bacteria levels in foods after processing. If bacteria levels are high, people who eat the food may get sick.

In processing plants, food technologists make sure that proper temperature and humidity levels are maintained in storage areas, wastes are disposed of properly, and other sanitary regulations are observed throughout the plant.

Some food technologists test new products in test kitchens or develop new processing methods in laboratory pilot plants. Others devise new methods for packaging and storing foods. They consult with processing engineers, flavor experts, and packaging and marketing specialists.

Food technologists work in laboratories, offices, and test kitchens and on production lines at food processing plants, food ingredient plants, and food manufacturing plants. Most are employed in private industry, but some work for government agencies, such as the Environmental Protection Agency, the Food and Drug Administration, and the U.S. Department of Agriculture.

Education and Training

To prepare for a career as a food technologist, take plenty of high school science courses. Be sure to take biology, chemistry, and physics. To get hands-on experience working with food, take family and consumer science classes. Four years of math classes, English classes, computer science classes, and other college preparatory courses are also important to take.

DID YOU KNOW?

- There are more than 250 types of food-borne diseases.
- There are 76 million cases of food-borne disease in the United States each year.
- Approximately 325,000 of these cases require hospitalization.
- Five thousand people die each year from food-borne disease.

Source: Centers for Disease Control and Prevention

Words to Learn

food-borne illness sickness resulting from eating food that is contaminated by bacteria, viruses, parasites, amoebas, and other biological and chemical agents

microorganism a microscopic animal or plant-like organism

organism a living being

pasteurization the heating of food under controlled cir-

cumstances in order to destroy pathogenic microorganisms

pathogen a microorganism that is capable of causing disease

sterilization a process in food production where all harmful life forms (bacteria, viruses, etc.) are destroyed

Source: Institute of Food Technologists

FOR MORE INFO

For consumer fact sheets, information on issues in the food science industry, and food safety news, visit the association's Web site or contact

Grocery Manufacturers Association
1350 I Street, NW
Washington, DC 20005-3377
202-639-5900
info@gmaonline.org
http://www.gmaonline.org

For information on accredited food science programs and to read *Introduction to the Food Industry and Food Science & Technology*, visit the IFT Web site.

Institute of Food Technologists (IFT)
525 West Van Buren, Suite 1000
Chicago, IL 60607-3830

312-782-8424
info@ift.org
http://www.ift.org

For national news on agriculture and food issues, contact

U.S. Department of Agriculture
1400 Independence Avenue, SW
Washington, DC 20250-0002
202-720-2791
http://www.usda.gov

For information on food safety, contact

U.S. Food and Drug Administration
10903 New Hampshire Avenue
Silver Spring, MD 20993-0002
888-463-6332
http://www.fda.gov

Food technologists need at least a bachelor's degree in food technology, food science, or food engineering. Some technologists have degrees in chemistry, biology, engineering, agriculture, or business. Master's degrees and doctorates are usually necessary for jobs in management or for research and teaching positions.

Undergraduate programs in food technology usually include courses in physics, biochemistry, mathematics, biology, the social sciences, humanities, and business administration in addition to food technology courses, such as food preservation, processing, sanitation, and marketing.

Earnings

Food technologists earned annual median salaries of $60,180 in 2010. Those just starting out in the field earned less than $35,000. Very experienced workers made $106,000 or more.

Outlook

The food industry is the largest single industry in the United States and throughout the world. People are always interested in trying new and different food products. This will create a demand for food scientists and technologists.

Several factors have also created continuing demand for skilled technologists. Food labeling laws require companies to provide detailed nutritional information on their products, such as the amount of fat or salt. The trend toward more healthy eating habits has encouraged companies to create a variety of low-fat, low-carb, low-sodium, fat-free, cholesterol-free, and sodium-free foods.

Food technologists will also be sought to produce new foods for poor and starving people in underdeveloped countries. Experienced technologists will use their advanced training to create new foods from such staples as rice, corn, wheat, and soybeans.

Food Writers and Editors

What Food Writers and Editors Do

Food writers and editors deal with the written word, whether the completed work is the printed page, broadcast, or computer screen. They tend to write about or edit all things related to food and beverages. This includes recipes, new food products, meal planning and preparation, grocery shopping, cooking utensils and related products, and places that serve food and beverages. The nature of their work is as varied as the materials they produce: magazines, newspapers, books, trade journals and other publications, text for Web sites, advertisements, and scripts for radio and television broadcast. The one common factor is the subject: food.

Food writers need to be able to write very descriptively, since the reader will not be able to taste, touch, or smell the product they are writing about. Depending on whether or not pictures or videos accompany the written word, the reader may not even be able to see it. Food writers use their writing skills to write about many different things. They might write a press release about a new food product to be distributed to food editors at numerous newspapers and magazines. They may write a story about seasonal fruits and vegetables for a local television news broadcast. They may write an article for a women's magazine about new cooking utensils that make meal preparation easier for amateur chefs. They may write a review about a new restaurant that just opened.

Perhaps the most infamous type of food writer is the *food/restaurant critic.* The critic needs to be fair with any type of

EXPLORING

- Explore your passion for food and increase your knowledge by taking cooking classes, attending ethnic festivals and food events, or touring different food-related businesses.
- Experiment with different types of restaurants and cuisines. After dining at a new restaurant, write about the experience.
- As a high school or college student, explore your interest in the fields of writing and editing by working as a reporter or writer on school newspapers, yearbooks, and literary magazines.
- Professional organizations dedicated to food writing and editing, such as those listed at the end of this article, often provide information, resources, conferences, and other guidance programs that may be of interest to you.
- Ask a teacher or counselor to arrange an information interview with a food writer or editor.

product or restaurant review. When dining at a restaurant, he or she also needs to be anonymous (hide their identity), which is not always easy. While dining, food/restaurant critics need to make accurate observations and try to write or record them without arousing the suspicion of the restaurant staff, lest they realize they were being reviewed and adjust the level of service or quality.

Food editors need to be able to polish the work of a food writer into a finished article or book. They correct grammar, spelling, and style. They check all the facts, especially where recipes are concerned. Editors make sure that the writing adheres to style guidelines, and that the writing is appropriate for the intended audience. When working for a magazine or

DID YOU KNOW?

Where Food Writers and Editors Work

- Book publishers
- Food/beverage manufacturing companies
- Food/beverage trade associations
- Magazines
- Newspapers
- Online publications
- Self-employment
- Television and radio stations

newspaper, food editors may also plan the editorial content of an entire food section. This section may range in size from as little as half of a page to a multiple-page spread. Their duties may include assigning stories to staff or freelance writers, as well as assigning photography or artwork assignments as needed, to accompany the articles and recipes.

Food writers and editors who work for publishing houses may work on tour or guidebooks. They write and edit restaurant reviews and stories about regional food specialties. Or they may work with recipes and cookbooks, carefully checking to ensure all ingredients and measurements are correct, and that no steps have been left out from the cooking directions.

Education and Training

If you are interested in becoming a food writer or an editor, take English, general science, home economics, and computer classes while in high school. If they are offered, take classes in writing or editing, such as journalism and business communications. Writers and editors must be expert communicators, so you should excel in English. You must learn to write well, since you will be correcting and even rewriting the work of others. While in high school, working on your school's newspaper, yearbook, or any other publication will be of benefit to you.

Most food writing and editing jobs require a college education. Some employers want new hires to have communications or journalism degrees. Others require culinary course work or even a degree in culinary arts. Most schools offer courses in journalism and some have more specialized courses in book publishing, publication management, and newspaper and magazine writing. Some offer majors or minors in food writing.

Some employers require a degree or certificate from culinary school, or culinary work experience, in addition to a background in writing or editing. You may wish to take cooking classes at a local culinary school or community college to improve your chances of landing a job as a food writer or editor.

Earnings

The International Association of Culinary Professionals compiled a list of median salaries for careers in the culinary field, including the following: cookbook author, $5,000 to $10,000 for their first book; cookbook editor, $27,000 to $85,000 annually; magazine food editor, $41,000 to $80,000 annually; newspaper food editor, $39,000 to $61,000 annually; food writer on staff at a publication, $19,000 to $40,000 annually; and freelance food writer, $100 to $1,000 per story. In general, salaries are higher in large cities. Salaries also depend on the employer, as larger publications tend to pay more, and the writer's or editor's level of experience, as those with many years of experience are able to earn a larger salary.

In addition to their salaries, many food writers and editors receive additional compensation. Most food critics, for example, have the meals they eat at a restaurant for the purpose of a review paid for by their employer. Some food writers and editors also receive travel expenses to cover expenditures such as mileage from driving to cover local events, or airfare and hotel accommodations for covering out-of-town industry events.

Food Magazines on the Web

Bon Appetit
http://www.bonappetit.com

Cook's Illustrated
http://www.cooksillustrated.com

Fine Cooking
http://www.finecooking.com

Gourmet
http://www.gourmet.com

FOR MORE INFO

Visit this organization's Web site for information on issues facing food writers and editors.

Association of Food Journalists
7 Avenida Vista Grande, Suite B7, #467
Santa Fe, NM 87508-9207
http://www.afjonline.com

For information on the magazine industry, contact

Association of Magazine Media
810 Seventh Avenue, 24th Floor
New York, NY 10019-5873
212-872-3700
mpa@magazine.org
http://www.magazine.org

For information on the newspaper industry, contact

Dow Jones Newspaper Fund
PO Box 300
Princeton, NJ 08543-0300
609-452-2820

djnf@dowjones.com
https://www.newsfund.org

This organization provides a wealth of industry information at its Web site.

International Association of Culinary Professionals
1100 Johnson Ferry Road, Suite 300
Atlanta, GA 30342-1733
404-252-3663
info@iacp.com
http://www.iacp.com

This organization offers an online newsletter and magazine at its Web site.

International Food, Wine & Travel Writers Association
1142 South Diamond Bar Boulevard, #177
Diamond Bar, CA 91765-2203
877-439-8929
admin@ifwtwa.org
http://www.ifwtwa.org

Outlook

Employment for all writers and editors is expected to be good during the next decade. Employment will not be as strong for food writers and editors. Individuals entering this field should realize that the competition for jobs is intense. Students just out of college may especially have trouble finding employment. However, the subject of food and beverages continues to grow in popularity, thus providing more opportunities for those who wish to pursue a career in food writing and editing.

Grain Merchants

What Grain Merchants Do

If you have ever had pasta, bread, or oatmeal, you have eaten grain. Grain is an edible seed that is used in countless types of foods. Examples of grains include wheat, oats, rice, cornmeal, and barley.

Grain merchants take the grain grown by farmers and deliver it to the public. They are necessary because people need grain year-round, but farmers can harvest only when the grain is ripe. So grain merchants buy, store, inspect, process, and transport the raw grain. This ensures that there is always enough to meet the public's needs, regardless of shortages and surpluses.

Grain merchants may work independently if they have enough money, but many merchants work for grain corporations or farmer-owned cooperatives. In either case, there are two major specialists who perform different functions in this occupation.

Grain buyers evaluate and buy grain for resale and milling (grinding). They select the type of grains

EXPLORING

- Learn more about the different types of grain by reading books and visiting Web sites.
- If you live in a grain-growing area, take a tour of a county or terminal elevator.
- If you live in a city, take a tour of a commodities exchange or meet with a grain broker.
- Joining the National FFA Organization or a 4-H Club will teach you about current agricultural issues.

Tips for Success

To be a successful grain merchant, you should

- get along well with farmers and other suppliers; this will help you get a good price on the grain, favorable payment terms, quick delivery on emergency orders, or help in obtaining the grain during times of shortage
- have good communication skills
- work well under pressure
- be persuasive, diplomatic, and cooperative
- have good judgment
- be dependable and trustworthy

to order based on current demand and possible future considerations. They arrange for the transportation and storage of the grain and also identify possible resale markets. Grain buyers may buy and store grain directly from the farmer, or they may work in a large terminal elevator in such grain centers as Chicago, Minneapolis, or Kansas City. *Terminal elevator buyers* get their grain from county elevators (where grain is stored) rather than directly from the farmer. Other buyers work for food processors, selecting the right type of grain for their products.

Grain managers work at terminal elevators or other holding facilities. They inspect all the grain that comes to the holding terminal and calculate its market value (the price people or organizations will pay for it). They may also send samples to federal grain inspection agencies for a government standardized analysis. As managers of local or county grain elevators, they keep daily records on the kinds and grades of grain received, prices paid, amounts purchased, and the amount in storage. They also supervise grain elevator workers.

Many grain merchants travel in the course of their work. As they learn about different kinds of markets and firms, they may change jobs several times. Those working in this field must learn all they can about the grain market. This includes knowledge of weather, crop size and quality, transportation and storage costs, government regulations and policies, and supply and demand—whatever might affect grain and grain prices.

Education and Training

In high school, take classes in agriculture, business, math, and science. Although you may be able to get some assistant positions with only a high school diploma, many grain merchants have undergraduate or graduate degrees in agriculture, economics, or business management from a college or university. However, two-year programs are also available and can open many doors for you.

Many students get summer jobs at a grain elevator while they are still in school, and then they are hired at full-time positions when they graduate. Others may begin work as a clerk or runner in a brokerage or grain merchant firm and then work their way up to becoming a broker or buyer. Still others work for state and federal government agencies, where their responsibilities include making inspections, seeing that regulations are met, and granting warehouse and broker licenses.

Earnings

As with other brokers, some grain merchants work on a commission basis and others work for a straight salary. Earnings vary depending on the

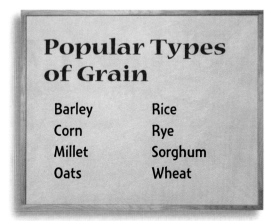

Popular Types of Grain

Barley	Rice
Corn	Rye
Millet	Sorghum
Oats	Wheat

FOR MORE INFO

Organizations such as 4-H and the National FFA Organization (formerly Future Farmers of America) offer good opportunities for learning about, visiting, and participating in farming activities.

4-H Clubs
7100 Connecticut Avenue
Chevy Chase, MD 20815-4934
301-961-2800
info@fourhcouncil.edu
http://www.4h-usa.org

National FFA Organization
6060 FFA Drive
PO Box 68960
Indianapolis, IN 46268-0960
317-802-6060
http://www.ffa.org

To learn about current issues affecting grain companies and their employees, contact
Grain Elevator and Processing Society
4248 Park Glen Road
Minneapolis, MN 55416-4758
952-928-4640
info@geaps.com
http://www.geaps.com

To learn about the federal government's role in the marketing of grain, contact
Grain Inspection, Packers, and Stockyards Administration
1400 Independence Avenue, SW
Stop 3601, Room 2055–South Building
Washington, DC 20250-3601
202-720-0219
http://www.gipsa.usda.gov

size of the employer, the experience of the employee, and the specific job responsibilities. Beginning grain merchants can expect to earn $20,000 to $31,000 a year. Experienced grain merchants earn between $54,000 and $101,000 annually.

Outlook

Little change is expected in the employment of purchasing agents and buyers of farm products during the next decade. It is often difficult to predict how successful this industry will be each year because changes in the weather, economy, and government affect growth in this field.

The populations of small agricultural communities are declining rapidly in some parts of the country, particularly in the

Plains states. However, even though many of the grain elevators are closing in these areas as farmers look for more stable sources of income, grain is still in great demand around the world. Agribusiness professionals, consultants, and the U.S. government are all involved in increasing this demand by searching for new, efficient uses for grain. Scientific advances will also aid in the storage and processing of grain.

Personal Chefs

What Personal Chefs Do

Personal chefs prepare menus for individuals and their families. They buy the ingredients for the meals, then cook, package, and store the meals in the clients' own kitchens. They usually charge a per-meal fee to prepare enough meals to last a few days or a few weeks.

EXPLORING

- Spend time in the kitchen. Learn how to properly use the cooking appliances and utensils.
- Experiment with recipes. Search the Web for sites with recipes that are good to freeze and store.
- Cook for friends and family, and volunteer to work at school or church banquets and dinners.
- Talk to a personal chef about his or her career.

Personal chefs first meet with clients to discuss special dietary needs and food preferences. Some clients require vegetarian and low-fat cooking. Others have diabetes or swallowing disorders that require special consideration. From these specifications, personal chefs prepare a menu. On the day that they cook the meals, they visit the grocery store to purchase fresh meats, fish, fruits, and vegetables. At the home of the client, they prepare the meals, package them, label them, and put them in the freezer. Depending on the number of meals, personal chefs spend anywhere from three to eight hours in their clients' kitchens.

Most personal chefs prepare the meals in clients' kitchens to avoid the requirements of licensing their own kitchens for commercial use. However, some chefs choose to operate commercial kitchens and provide catering services as well as personal chef services.

Personal chefs know about meals and ingredients that can be easily frozen and reheated without hurting taste and appearance. They have an understanding of nutrition, health, and sanitation. They spend some time testing recipes, trying out equipment, and looking for the stores that offer quality groceries at the lowest price. Personal chefs also need good business sense. They must keep financial records, market their service, create schedules, and bill clients.

Most personal chefs try to confine their services to their local areas or neighborhoods to keep travel from kitchen to kitchen at a minimum.

Education and Training

Family and consumer science courses are a good beginning to a career in food preparation. You'll learn about cooking, budgeting for groceries, and how to use cooking equipment and appliances. Courses in health and nutrition are recommended.

A formal education isn't required of personal chefs, but a good culinary school can give you valuable cooking experience. Culinary programs include courses in baking, soups and sauces, meats, vegetables and fruits, vegetarian cooking, menu design, and food safety and sanitation along with courses such as economics and math.

The American Personal & Private Chef Association and the United States Personal Chef Association offer self-study courses and seminars on the personal chef business. These courses teach you how to start a service, how to market it, how much to charge for services, and other concerns specific to the personal

A personal chef plates a client's meal. (C. H. Pete Copeland, AP Photo/ *The Plain Dealer*)

Tips for Success

To be a successful personal chef, you should

- have an outgoing personality
- have a strong work ethic
- be a good businessperson
- have excellent cooking skills
- be creative
- have a passion for cooking

chef business. These courses also offer recipes for foods that freeze and store well.

Earnings

According to the United States Personal Chef Association, salaries for personal chefs range from about $35,000 annually on the low end to $50,000 on the high end. Some chefs with assistant cooks and a number of clients can make much more, but businesses composed of a single owner/operator average about $40,000 per year. The U.S. Department of Labor reported earnings for cooks in private households of between $17,000 and $46,000 annually in 2010.

Outlook

There should continue to be good opportunities for personal chefs. The career has become recognized by culinary institutes, and some schools are beginning to include personal chef courses as part of their curriculums.

Personal chefs will need to keep up with diet and cooking trends and new health concerns. Those with experience

DID YOU KNOW?

- It is estimated that there are 9,000 personal chefs. They serve 72,000 clients.
- Personal chefs generally earn $200 to $500 a day.
- The American Culinary Federation accredits more than 200 postsecondary culinary training programs.

Sources: American Personal & Private Chef Association, American Culinary Federation

FOR MORE INFO

For industry information, contact
AIB International
PO Box 3999
Manhattan, KS 66505-3999
785-537-4750
http://www.aibonline.org

For information on apprenticeships and culinary trends, contact
American Culinary Federation Inc.
180 Center Place Way
St. Augustine, FL 32095-8859
800-624-9458
acf@acfchefs.net
http://www.acfchefs.org

For information on culinary education, contact
American Hotel and Lodging Educational Institute
800 North Magnolia Avenue, Suite 1800
Orlando, FL 32803-3271
800-752-4567
http://www.ahlei.org

For information on a career as a personal chef, contact
American Personal & Private Chef Association
4572 Delaware Street
San Diego, CA 92116-1005

800-644-8389
info@personalchef.com
http://www.personalchef.com

For information on educational programs, including classes for kids, contact
The Culinary Institute of America
1946 Campus Drive
Hyde Park, NY 12538-1430
845-452-9600
http://www.ciachef.edu

This organization provides a wealth of industry information at its Web site.
International Association of Culinary Professionals
1100 Johnson Ferry Road, Suite 300
Atlanta, GA 30342-1733
404-252-3663
info@iacp.com
http://www.iacp.com

The USPCA offers training courses and mentorship opportunities.
United States Personal Chef Association (USPCA)
5728 Major Boulevard, Suite 750
Orlando, FL 32819-7963
800-995-2138
http://www.uspca.com

and creativity in regard to preparing new recipes will have the best job prospects.

Restaurant and Food Service Managers

What Restaurant and Food Service Managers Do

Have you ever been to a restaurant with your parents? Was the service really good—meaning did you get your food quickly and did it taste great? If so, one of the workers you can thank for this experience is the manager.

Restaurant and food service managers are responsible for the overall operation of restaurants and other establishments that serve food. Managers usually hire and train their workers. Restaurant and food service managers buy the food and equipment necessary for the operation of the restaurant or facility. They may help with menu planning. They inspect the restaurant kitchen and food storage areas to make sure that they are clean and safe and meet government health regulations. Restaurant and food service managers perform many clerical and financial duties, such as keeping records, directing payroll operations, handling large sums of money, and keeping track of supplies. Managers also usually supervise advertising and special sales programs.

Restaurant and food service managers often talk with customers. They take suggestions, handle complaints, and try to create a friendly atmosphere in which diners can enjoy themselves. If a customer has a problem with the food or service, the manager offers to fix it. If the diner offers a suggestion on how to improve the restaurant, the manager listens to the customer's advice and, if possible, works to make the restaurant better.

EXPLORING

- You can learn about food preparation and food service by getting involved in planning and budgeting for family, religious, or community events that involve food. Try to participate in every aspect of such events, including cooking, assigning tasks to others, buying ingredients and supplies, organizing dining areas, and hosting.
- Visit a restaurant and observe the many different types of workers—including the manager—that it takes to keep things operating efficiently.
- Ask your teacher or parent to set up a presentation by a restaurant or food service manager. Be prepared with questions such as the following: How did you train for this field? What are the pros and cons of your job? What advice would you give to someone who is interested in this field?

Very large restaurants may employ *assistant managers,* an *executive chef, food and beverage managers,* and a *wine steward* in addition to restaurant and food service managers. These workers are trained to supervise the kitchen staff. They also are responsible for all food and drink preparation in the restaurant.

In some cases, the manager of a restaurant is also its owner. The *owner-manager* of a restaurant is likely to be involved in service functions. They sometimes operate the cash register, wait on tables, and do a wide variety of tasks. *Nonowner-managers* of large restaurants or institutional food service facilities are usually employees who are paid a salary. They may work in dining rooms and cafeterias of hotels, department stores, factories, schools, hospitals, ships, trains, and private clubs.

Education and Training

You need to have experience in all areas of restaurant and food service work before you can advance to the level of manager. You must be familiar with food preparation, food service, sanitary rules, and financial operations. Managers also must have good business skills in order to manage a budget and a staff. They apply this business knowledge as they buy machinery, equipment, and food.

Programs in restaurant and hospitality management or institutional food service management are offered by nearly 1,000 colleges and universities. These programs combine classroom work with on-the-job experience. Some graduates of technical or vocational schools can quickly qualify for management training.

Some managers learn their skills through a special apprenticeship program sponsored by the National Restaurant Association. Many restaurant and food service managers start as waiters or kitchen staff. As they gain on-the-job experience, they take on more responsibility and eventually move into management positions.

Earnings

Salaries of restaurant and food service managers vary depending on size of the facility, location, and amount of business. Food service managers earned median salaries of $48,130 in 2010, according to the U.S. Department of Labor (DOL). Salaries ranged from less than $31,000 to $80,000 or more annually. In general, large restaurants in and around cities pay the highest salaries. Mean annual earnings for managers of full-service restau-

DID YOU KNOW?

- There are approximately 338,700 restaurant and food service managers in the United States.
- Forty-one percent of managers work in full-service restaurants or limited-service eating places, such as cafeterias and fast-food restaurants.
- Restaurant and food service managers typically work more than 50 hours a week.

Source: U.S. Department of Labor

Earnings by Industry, 2010

TYPE OF EMPLOYER	MEAN ANNUAL EARNINGS
General medical and surgical hospitals	$70,140
Traveler accommodations	$60,650
Full-service restaurants	$54,160
Elementary and secondary schools	$50,180
Limited-service eating places	$46,070

Source: U.S. Department of Labor

rants were $54,160 in 2010, according to the DOL. In addition to a base salary, most managers receive bonuses based on profits, which can range from $2,000 to $7,500 a year.

Outlook

Employment for restaurant and food service managers will be good during the next decade. Many job openings will arise from the need to replace managers retiring from the workforce. Also, population growth will result in an increased demand for eating establishments. Managers who have earned bachelor's or associate's degrees in restaurant management or related areas will have the best employment prospects.

Economic downswings have a great effect on eating and drinking establishments. During a recession (a time of poor economic conditions), people have less money to spend on luxuries such as dining out, thus hurting the restaurant business. However, greater numbers of working parents and their families are finding it convenient to eat out or purchase carryout food from a restaurant.

FOR MORE INFO

For information on accredited education programs, contact

International Council on Hotel, Restaurant, and Institutional Education
2810 North Parham, Suite 230
Richmond, VA 23294-4422
804-346-4800
http://www.chrie.org

For information on training, contact

International Food Service Executives Association
4955 Miller Street, Suite 107
Wheat Ridge, CO 80033-2294
800-893-5499
hq@ifsea.com
http://www.ifsea.com

For information on education and careers, contact

National Restaurant Association Educational Foundation
175 West Jackson Boulevard, Suite 1500
Chicago, IL 60604-2702
800-765-2122
http://www.nraef.org

For information on career opportunities in Canada, contact

Canadian Restaurant and Foodservices Association
316 Bloor Street West
Toronto, ON M5S 1W5 Canada
800-387-5649
info@crfa.ca
http://www.crfa.ca

Supermarket Managers

What Supermarket Managers Do

Supermarkets are busy places. In a typical day, thousands of customers walk the aisles and visit the various departments. A variety of people work as cashiers, stock clerks, and in other positions in these departments. *Supermarket managers* supervise these workers and help run the daily operations of grocery stores. Managers include store managers, assistant store managers, courtesy booth/service desk managers, customer service

EXPLORING

- Visit http://www.fmi.org/glossary to read a glossary of supermarket terms.
- Hang out at your local store. Go on a busy day and a slow one. Study what activities are taking place and how management's role changes from day to day. Get a feel for the pace to decide if you would want to spend a lot of hours in a retail atmosphere.

- If you are interested in becoming a supermarket manager, get a job at a supermarket. Any job, from bagger to cashier, will help you understand the industry better.
- Interview supermarket managers to discuss the things they like and do not like about their jobs.

managers, receiving managers, and managers of such departments as bakery, deli/food service, food court, front end, grocery, meat/seafood, frozen foods, pharmacy, and produce/floral. The size and location of the store determines how many of these management levels exist in each store. In a small, family-owned grocery, the manager and owner may be the same person.

Supermarket managers work with employees and customers all day. They are in charge of the business aspects of the store, including budgets, scheduling, and inventory. Each store may employ 250 or more people, so skill in interviewing, hiring, and managing workers is very important.

Supermarket managers supervise many types of workers, including cashiers, clerks, baggers, stock personnel, butchers, bakers, deli workers, janitors and cleaners, human resource professionals, accounting professionals, security workers, advertising and marketing workers, information technology professionals, public relations professionals, and pharmacists and pharmacy technicians (at larger chain supermarkets that have a pharmacy).

Planning is an important part of the supermarket manager's job. Supermarket managers plan promotions and budgets while also setting up holiday promotions and displays. Because some grocery stores are open 24 hours a day, managers may work different schedules each week. They often work late hours, weekends, and holidays.

To be a successful supermarket manager, you should have excellent communication and management skills. You should

DID YOU KNOW?

- The first supermarket, King Kullen Grocery Company, opened in New York in 1930.
- Saturday is the most popular day for shopping. The next most popular days? Sunday and Friday.
- There are 35,612 supermarkets ($2 million or more in annual sales) in the United States.
- The average consumer makes two trips to the supermarket each week.
- The average number of items carried in a supermarket is 46,852.
- The average family spends $91.90 each week on groceries.

Source: Food Marketing Institute

be able to get along well with people and handle customer service issues. You should be able to work in sometimes hectic and stressful work conditions. Other important traits include good organizational skills, the ability to think on your feet to solve problems, and strong business skills.

Education and Training

In high school, you should take English, business, speech, computer science, and math classes to help you prepare for supermarket work. Classes in marketing, advertising, or statistics will also be helpful.

You will need at least a high school diploma to work in this field. While a college degree is not always necessary, there is a trend toward hiring new managers straight out of college. Many people work through the ranks of a grocery store to become a manager, but it has recently become popular to hire managers who have college degrees in business or retail management. Even an associate's degree in retail or business management will give you an advantage over other applicants who have only a high school diploma.

Largest Supermarket and Grocery Store Chains (by 2010 grocery sales)

1. Wal-Mart Stores
2. Kroger Co.
3. Costco Wholesale Corp.
4. Safeway
5. Supervalu
6. Loblaw Cos.
7. Publix Super Markets
8. Ahold USA
9. C&S Wholesale Grocers
10. Delhaize America

Source: *Supermarket News*

FOR MORE INFO

For industry-related statistics, contact
Food Marketing Institute
2345 Crystal Drive, Suite 800
Arlington, VA 22202-4813
202-452-8444
http://www.fmi.org

For general information on retail industries, contact the following organizations:
National Retail Federation
325 7th Street, NW, Suite 1100
Washington, DC 20004-2825

800-673-4692
http://www.nrf.com

Retail Industry Leaders Association
1700 North Moore Street, Suite 2250
Arlington, VA 22209-1933
703-841-2300
http://www.rila.org

Earnings

According to the U.S. Department of Labor, grocery store managers earned mean annual salaries of $39,130 in 2010. First-line su-
pervisors/managers of retail workers earned salaries that ranged
from less than $23,000 to $60,000 or more. In general, starting
managers can expect to make $30,000 a year. Department man-
agers at large stores average $50,000 annually. District managers
earn average salaries of $100,000 or more annually. These salary
numbers may include bonuses that are standard in the industry.
Pay is affected by management level, the size of the store, and the
location.

Outlook

Little or no employment growth is expected for supermarket
managers during the next decade. While the number of stores
(and managers needed to run them) is decreasing, specialization and demand will create the need for the best-trained and
most knowledgeable managers.

Winemakers

What Winemakers Do

Wine is an alcoholic beverage that people age 21 and over can drink legally. Enology, better known as winemaking, is more than 5,000 years old. It is one of the world's oldest professions. The ancient Egyptians, Greeks, Romans, and Chinese all used wine for either medicinal or religious purposes or just to drink with a meal. Grapes for winemaking have been grown in the United States since the late 1800s. Winemaking here is now a major industry, especially in California, where more than 80 percent of U.S. wines are produced.

Winemakers, sometimes called *enologists,* are involved in all phases of wine production and must have a thorough understanding of the business. As an expert in viticulture (the growing of grapes), the enologist has many important decisions to make. Perhaps the most important decision is which grapes to grow. There are thousands of types of grapes, and they differ in color, size, shape, and flavor. Winemakers study the different European and American grapes and then decide which varieties are best for the soil and climate of their land. For example, a winemaker in the Napa Valley of California needs to make sure the grapes planted can withstand very hot summers, while in upstate New York, grapes need to survive extremely cold winters. Different varieties of grapes have different planting, pruning, and harvesting times.

Winemakers must keep up to date on all of the new technology that comes along to help the winemaking process. For ex-

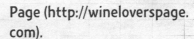

EXPLORING

- Read books about winemaking and a career as a winemaker.
- Visit Web sites about winemaking. Here are two suggestions: Professional Friends of Wine: Wine History (http://www.winepros.org/wine101/history.htm) and WineLovers Page (http://wineloverspage.com).
- Take a tour of a winery and watch winemakers in action.
- Ask your teacher or parent to arrange an information interview with someone who works in a winery.

ample, winemakers might have to decide whether to use highly mechanical grape harvesters and crushers, which speed up the entire winemaking process but might affect the quality. The winemaker also has to consult with staff members about the testing and crushing of the grapes and their cooling, filtering, and bottling.

As the business managers of a winery, winemakers must be organized and knowledgeable in financial matters. For example, they must have the ability to analyze financial documents and records such as profit-and-loss statements and balance sheets. Winemakers are also involved with the marketing of the wines. This includes making such crucial decisions as where the wines will be sold and at what price. They usually oversee all matters involving their staffs, including hiring, firing, and setting salaries. Winemakers are top-level managers who have final responsibility for the success of their wineries.

A dedication to winemaking and an understanding of chemistry are important characteristics of winemakers. An interest in constantly learning new things is an advantage in this field.

A winemaker stirs a vat of grapes. (Jeff Greenberg, The Image Works)

Education and Training

To prepare for a career in this field, take courses in biology, chemistry, and other sciences in high school. Business, economics, marketing, and computer science classes will also be useful.

Winemaking is an increasingly competitive field, and you will likely need a college degree to obtain an entry-level job. In college, you should major in viticulture or horticulture. Some wineries offer on-the-job training in the form of apprenticeship for high school graduates. However, most entry-level positions go to college graduates, so a college degree is recommended.

Tips for Success

To be a successful winemaker, you should

- have excellent verbal and written communication skills
- be able to handle multiple tasks and priorities
- be able to take direction from supervisors and work well on a team
- have basic computer knowledge
- have a familiarity with the Bureau of Alcohol, Tobacco, Firearms, and Explosives and state regulations concerning winemaking, handling, and transport.
- have the physical strength to climb stairs, work on high platforms, lift and carry 40 pounds, bend, squat, and stretch
- be at least 21 years of age

Advancement within the profession depends on a combination of education, experience, and skill. Winemakers at small wineries may move on to become managers of large ones, and they in turn may become directors of several wineries that are part of a large corporation. Because of the small number of wineries, however, and because enologists are already high-level managers, opportunities for advancement are limited.

Earnings

Beginning salary levels for winemakers depend on the applicant's education level

DID YOU KNOW?

The people of France drink the most wine. Following is a list of some of the top wine-drinking countries in the world:

- Argentina
- China
- France
- Germany
- Italy
- Romania
- Russia
- Spain
- United Kingdom
- United States

Source: U.S. Department of Commerce, 2008

FOR MORE INFO

For industry information, contact
American Society for Enology and Viticulture
PO Box 1855
Davis, CA 95617-1855
530-753-3142
http://asev.org

For industry information, contact
American Wine Society
PO Box 279
Englewood, OH 45322-0279
888-297-9070
http://www.americanwinesociety.org

and the size of the winery. A survey of the wine industry by *Wine Business Monthly* in 2010 reports that salaries ranged from a low of $20,000 for unskilled workers in the cellar or vineyard to highs of more than $200,000 for top winemakers and other executives at some larger wineries. Average salaries listed for enologists ranged from $52,000 to $64,000, depending on the size of the establishment.

Outlook

Job growth is tied to the size and quality of grape harvests, the success of wine production, and the demand for American wines in the United States and in other countries. Technological advances in wine production may create more job opportunities.

Although a wine producer may have an excellent harvest one year, they may have a bad year the next due to poor weather or other factors. In short, it is impossible to predict weather and soil conditions from season to season, and there is little security, especially for smaller wine producers. There is stiff competition in the wine business, and there have been a number of consolidations and mergers in the past few years. Still, new brands continue to be introduced with strong marketing campaigns, particularly in the lower and mid-priced categories. Wine exports (wine that is sold to other countries) are increasing, which means that there will be more opportunities for winemakers.

Job opportunities will be best in California, where most of the U.S. wineries are located. Most California wine is cultivated in the San Joaquin, Napa, and Sonoma valleys, the central coast, and the Sierra foothills.

Glossary

accredited   approved as meeting established standards for providing good training and education; this approval is usually given by an independent organization of professionals

annual salary   the money an individual earns for an entire year of work

apprentice   a person who is learning a trade by working under the supervision of a skilled worker; apprentices often receive classroom instruction in addition to their supervised practical experience

associate's degree   an academic rank or title granted by a community or junior college or similar institution to graduates of a two-year program of education beyond high school

bachelor's degree   an academic rank or title given to a person who has completed a four-year program of study at a college or university; also called an **undergraduate degree** or **baccalaureate**

career   an occupation for which a worker receives training and has an opportunity for advancement

certified   approved as meeting established requirements for skill, knowledge, and experience in a particular field; people are certified by an organization of professionals in their field

college   a higher education institution that is above the high school level

community college   a public or private two-year college attended by students who do not usually live at the college; graduates of a community college receive an associate's degree and may transfer to a four-year college or university to complete a bachelor's degree

diploma   a certificate or document given by a school to show that a person has completed a course or has graduated from the school

distance education   a type of educational program that allows students to take classes and complete their education by mail or the Internet

doctorate   the highest academic rank or title granted by a graduate school to a person who has completed a two- to three-year program after having received a master's degree

fellowship   a financial award given for research projects or dissertation assistance; fellowships are commonly offered at the graduate, postgraduate, or doctoral levels

freelancer   a worker who is not a regular employee of a company; they work for themselves and do not receive a regular paycheck

fringe benefit   a payment or benefit to an employee in addition to regular wages or salary; examples of fringe benefits include a pension, a paid vacation, and health or life insurance

graduate school   a school that people may attend after they have received their bachelor's degree; people who complete an educational program at a graduate school earn a master's degree or a doctorate

intern   an advanced student (usually one with at least some college training) in a professional field who is employed in a job that is intended to provide supervised practical experience for the student

internship   1. the position or job of an intern; 2. the period of time when a person is an intern

junior college   a two-year college that offers courses like those in the first half of a four-year college program; graduates of a junior college usually receive an associate's degree and may transfer to a four-year college or university to complete a bachelor's degree

liberal arts   the subjects covered by college courses that develop broad general knowledge rather than specific occupational skills; the liberal arts are often considered to include philosophy, literature and the arts, history, language, and some courses in the social sciences and natural sciences

major (in college)   the academic field in which a student specializes and receives a degree

master's degree   an academic rank or title granted by a graduate school to a person who has completed a one- or two-year program after having received a bachelor's degree

pension   an amount of money paid regularly by an employer to a former employee after he or she retires from working

scholarship   A gift of money to a student to help the student pay for further education

starting salary   salary paid to a newly hired employee; the starting salary is usually a smaller amount than is paid to a more experienced worker

technical college   a private or public college offering two- or four-year programs in technical subjects; technical colleges offer courses in both general and technical subjects and award associate's degrees and bachelor's degrees

undergraduate   a student at a college or university who has not yet received a degree

undergraduate degree   see **bachelor's degree**

union   an organization whose members are workers in a particular industry or company; the union works to gain better wages, benefits, and working conditions for its members; also called a **labor union** or **trade union**

vocational school   a public or private school that offers training in one or more skills or trades

wage   money that is paid in return for work done, especially money paid on the basis of the number of hours or days worked

Browse and Learn More

Books

Bijlefeld, Marjolijn, and Sharon K. Zoumbaris. *Food and You: A Guide to Healthy Habits for Teens.* Santa Barbara, Calif.: Greenwood Press, 2008.

Bowden, Rob. *Food Industry.* New York: Rosen Central, 2010.

Casper, Julie Kerr. *Agriculture: The Food We Grow and Animals We Raise.* New York: Chelsea House Publications, 2007.

Chalmers, Irena. *Food Jobs: 150 Great Jobs for Culinary Students, Career Changers and Food Lovers.* New York: Beaufort Books Inc., 2008.

Cunningham, Marion. *Cooking with Children: 15 Lessons for Children, Age 7 and Up, Who Really Want to Learn to Cook.* New York: Knopf, 1995.

D'Amico, Joan, and Karen Eich Drummond. *The Science Chef: 100 Fun Food Experiments and Recipes for Kids.* Hoboken, N.J.: Jossey-Bass, 1994.

———. *The United States Cookbook: Fabulous Foods and Fascinating Facts From All 50 States.* Hoboken, N.J.: Wiley, 2000.

Donovan, Mary. *Careers for Gourmets & Others Who Relish Food.* 2d ed. New York: McGraw-Hill, 2002.

Eddy, Jackie, and Ealeanor Clark. *The Absolute Beginner's Cookbook: Or, How Long Do I Cook a 3-Minute Egg?* New York: Prima Lifestyles, 2002.

Fernandez-Armesto, Felipe. *Near a Thousand Tables: A History of Food.* New York: Free Press, 2003.

Friedman, Lauri S. *Organic Food and Farming.* Farmington Hills, Mich.: Greenhaven Press, 2008.

Gold, Rozanne. *Kids Cook 1-2-3.* New York: Bloomsbury USA Children's Books, 2006.

Gold, Rozanne, and Phil Mansfield. *Eat Fresh Food: Awesome Recipes for Teen Chefs.* New York: Bloomsbury USA Children's Books, 2009.

Haduch, Bill, and Rick Stromoski. *Food Rules! The Stuff You Munch, Its Crunch, Its Punch, and Why You Sometimes Lose Your Lunch.* London, U.K.: Puffin Books, 2001.

Heyhoe, Kate. *Cooking with Kids For Dummies.* Hoboken, N.J.: For Dummies, 1999.

Kukathas, Uma. *Global Food Crisis.* Farmington Hills, Mich.: Greenhaven Press, 2009.

Langley, Andrew. *Is Organic Food Better?* Chicago: Heinemann Library, 2008.

Maynard, Chris. *Kitchen Science.* New York: DK Publishing Inc., 2001.

Meredith, Susan. *Science in the Kitchen.* Rev. ed. Atlanta, Ga.: Usborne Books, 2007.

Pasternak, Ceel, and Linda Thornburg. *Cool Careers for Girls in Food.* Manassas Park, Va.: Impact Publications, 1999.

Wilson, Charles, and Eric Schlosser. *Chew on This: Everything You Don't Want to Know About Fast Food.* New York: Sandpiper, 2007.

Periodicals

Better Homes and Gardens
http://www.bhg.com

Bon Appetit
http://www.bonappetit.com

Cook's Illustrated
http://www.cooksillustrated.com

Fine Cooking
http://www.finecooking.com

Gourmet
http://www.gourmet.com

Web Sites

4-H Clubs
http://www.4-h.org

Agriculture in the Classroom
http://www.agclassroom.org/kids

American Dietetic Association: It's About Eating Right
http://www.eatright.org/Public

American Library Association: Great Web Sites for Kids
http://www.ala.org/greatsites

Better Homes and Gardens: Baking Glossary
http://www.bhg.com/recipes/how-to/bake/baking-glossary

CIAkids.com
http://www.ciakids.com

Cookalotamus
http://www.cookalotamus.com

Cyber Space Farm
http://www.cyberspaceag.com

Farm Service Agency for Kids
http://www.fsa.usda.gov/FSA/kidsapp?area=home&subject=landing
&topic=landing

Food: A Fact of Life
http://www.foodafactoflife.org.uk

Food and Drug Administration Kids
http://www.fda.gov/ForConsumers/ByAudience/ForKids

The Food Museum Online
http://www.foodmuseum.com

Food Network.com
http://www.foodnetwork.com

Hershey's: Discover Hershey: Making Chocolate
http://www.thehersheycompany.com/about-hershey/our-story/mak-
ing-our-chocolate.aspx

Home Baking Association: Baking Glossary
http://www.homebaking.org/glossary/old_glossary.html

Kidnetic.com
http://www.kidnetic.com

Kids.gov
http://www.kids.gov

MyPyramid.gov
http://www.mypyramid.gov/kids

National FFA Organization
https://www.ffa.org

Nutrition Explorations
http://www.nutritionexplorations.org

Nutrition.gov
http://www.nutrition.gov

PBS: Empty Oceans, Empty Nets
http://www.pbs.org/emptyoceans

Professional Friends of Wine: Wine History
http://www.winepros.org/wine101/history.htm

Science of Cooking
http://www.exploratorium.edu/cooking

Spatulatta: Cooking 4 Kids Online
http://www.spatulatta.com

Thermy for Kids
http://www.fsis.usda.gov/food_safety_education/thermy_for_kids

Whole Foods Market: Nutrition for Kids & Teens
http://www.wholefoodsmarket.com/healthstartshere

WineLoversPage
http://wineloverspage.com

World of Food
http://www.topics-mag.com/foods/world-of-food.htm

Index